PURPOSEFUL LIVING

Melissa C. Roberts

Copyright © 2024 Melissa C. Roberts

All rights reserved.

No portion of this book may be reproduced, stored in a retrieval system, or transmitted in any form or by any means—electronic, mechanical, photocopy recording, scanning, or other—except for brief quotations without the prior written permission of the publisher..

Published by Write the Book Now, an imprint of Perfect Time SHP LLC.

ISBN: 979-8-9858585-5-6.

Table Of Contents

Chapter 1 _____ 5

   LOVING YOURSELF UNCONDITIONALLY _____ 5

Chapter 2 _____ 17

   WHOLENESS: LIVING A BALANCED LIFE: MIND, BODY, & SPIRIT _____ 17

Chapter 3 _____ 27

   WALK IN PURPOSE SACRIFICIALLY _____ 27

Chapter 4 _____ 36

   DISCOVER YOUR PURPOSE _____ 36

Chapter 5 _____ 47

   APPLICATION _____ 47

Chapter 6 _____ 55

   BECOME A BETTER COMMUNICATOR _____ 55

Chapter 7 _____ 65

   RELATIONSHIPS THAT FLOURISH _____ 65

Chapter 8 _____ 80

   FROM PROCESSING TO PROGRESSING _____ 80

Chapter 9 _____ 90

   SACRIFICIALLY WALKING IN PURPOSE _____ 90

Chapter 10 _____ *101*

    DIFFICULT CONVERSATIONS _____ 101

Chapter 11 _____ *110*

    MANAGING YOUR EMOTIONS _____ 110

Chapter 12 _____ *123*

    RUN YOUR RACE WITH CONFIDENCE _____ 123

About the Author _____ *131*

Chapter 1
LOVING YOURSELF UNCONDITIONALLY

You Are Enough and You Matter

"and in Him you have been made complete…" Colossians 2:10

You have unique gifts, talents, and abilities that are unique to you. Yes, they may resemble what someone else does, but how you deliver your gifts will always be different and uniquely yours if you don't try to copy someone else's. We are in a world where we are asked to look a certain way, act a certain way, and even show up a certain way, but it is not our job to mirror other's gifts. That's not what you were called to do. Actually, you are saying who God created you for is not enough when you work so hard to copy or even compare yourself to someone else.

With this understanding, the question is, can you show up great in what your assignment is? Sometimes this means you will stand alone and sometimes this may mean you will have others intimidated by your bravery and courage. Genesis 1:27 says, *"So God created man in his own image; he created him in the image of God; he created them male and female."* You were created by God as an image bearer. Which means, God is creative and so are you. With this being said, the gifts and purpose in you includes your ability to be creative. And being made in God's image, should help you to see your value and worth. Because of Creator God, you have exactly what you need to walk in purpose and love you with the same love and compassion God has for you and let that be enough.

You have been made complete (Colossians 2:10). So, rest in knowing you are enough and what you bring to the table is exactly what is needed. Look at your story and your life experiences. What you have been through is not who you are but has been added to your being. What you have been through adds to the spice you bring to the dish. What you have been through offers a totally different perspective and can be viewed through a different lens. Be confident in who you are and learn from your experiences, don't take on a new identity to fit that mold. Be bold in telling your story, by finding your voice, using it when asked to and scaling back when you need to.

Mind Your Tongue

"Death and life are in the power of the tongue." Proverbs 18:21

It is important to be aware how often you have negative conversations with yourself and with others. For you to make a mindset shift, you must first acknowledge the problem and have the willingness to change.

Negative conversations with self, won't completely be eliminated, because of our sinful nature and always being at war with the enemy of our souls. Intentional thoughts are very important. God tells us in Philippians 4:8-9, by *"fixing your thoughts"* then *"the God of peace will be with you."* Keep in mind, as you continue to learn and grow, you will be uncomfortable. The focus here is to make the necessary changes with your internal conversations and thoughts so you can live a life in peace. And not just any peace, but God's peace will be with you. When you have negative thoughts or limiting beliefs, train your brain to automatically think on things that are *"true, and honorable, and right, and pure, and lovely, and admirable. Think about things that are excellent and worthy of praise"* Philippians 4:8.

The more you feed positive thoughts to your mind, growth is bound to take place. Keep feeding your thoughts with intentional words of truth. It is appropriate for you to be a positive force of energy for yourself and not solely depend on someone else to do that for you. This won't happen overnight, but bad habits can be broken. You owe it to yourself and the ones you show up for, to get moving in the direction of intentional thinking.

Teach Others How to Love You

"Let no one look down on your youthfulness, but rather in speech, conduct, love, faith, and purity, show yourself an example of those who believe." 1 Timothy 4:12

It is important for you to set aside time to renew your mind and rest, and this is one way you can love yourself. In doing this, you will show others how to love you. I don't know anyone who is completely locked all in their purpose and is not consistently setting time aside for rest and recharge. How you rest, recharge, or renew depends on you knowing who you are and what you require to replenish what you have given out.

It is impossible to give from an empty well. Think about it this way, you have a bank account, when you go to the bank to withdraw, you expect something to be there that you can withdraw. If you never put anything in, if you never make a deposit, the teller is going to look at you in the most curious way and say, "Ma'am or Sir, you have withdrawn all of what you have put in and there is nothing left". Same principle here, you can't give out what you don't have. Remember, you were created by God in his image, so be like our Creator and rest after the "good" work is done.

In order to do this well, you need to know what replenishes you well. Knowing who you are is key in knowing how to truly replenish, refresh, and renew. In order to know you, you must know the God who created you. Taking the necessary time to know God and to "fear Him, He will make known his covenant" Psalms 25:14. Take time daily to read the manual that has been constructed for us to know God and to learn of his will for our lives. This will help because you will allow God to renew your mind and give you rest.

Times of rest and relaxation are important and when you are resting, be confident that if God wants you to complete a task or solve a problem for someone, He will make that evident , Life is to be enjoyed and the only way you will feel fulfilled and will get the full enjoyment out of life is if you are doing what you were created to do. The bible says, "for we are His workmanship, created in Christ Jesus for good works, which God prepared beforehand so that we would walk in them" Ephesians 2:10 NASB. We yearn to do the thing that completes us in such a way that we feel satisfied with life. When we know what that is and we do it, we feel valued completely because we value what we do and taking a rest will be good for you and the people you are serving

We are complete with satisfaction and joy, "we know that God causes all things to work together for good to those who love Him, to those who are called according to His purpose" Romans 8:28. Doing what you are called or purposed to do is one way you love yourself and love God.

When we love ourselves, we teach others how to love us in return. The way we teach others how to love us, is we model love. We model it in the way we speak about ourselves, how we speak about what we do, how we speak to others with kindness and respect, we emulate exactly what we want to receive. What we give, is what we will receive. It is an important skill to master. If you give love, you will receive love. If you give respect and honor, you will receive those in return. You get the picture. However, in order to love, you must be able to receive love and know love. Knowing love means you must know God because He is love (1 John 4:8).

Daily Gratitude Is Necessary

"In everything give thanks; for this is the will of God for you in Christ Jesus."

1 Thessalonians 5:18

Daily gratitude makes for a wonderful day walking out your purpose. "But seek first His kingdom and His righteousness, and all these things will be provided to you" (Matthew 6:33). Prioritize and make God first in your life. Make living righteously a priority, above all else seek God's righteousness and His kingdom and everything else will fall into place. You choose that moment in the day when your space is quiet and there are no distractions. Think about that time of the day when you can hear your thoughts and meditate on the grace that has been given to you by the Almighty God (Jeremiah 9:24). Grace means you and I didn't get what we deserved, unmerited favor. As you practice a life of gratitude, remember God's grace in your life and acknowledge how He has walked you through difficult times and sustained you..

Find that time and space for yourself and make it happen and see how this transforms your day. Focusing daily on what you are grateful for, brings a sense of clarity that one needs. Think about how to follow through on what you are responsible for and because your focus is clear, these things can be manifested in your life. You will have a clear focus and if your focus is clear, your actions will take shape and your behavior will follow what your mind is focused on producing. Committing your actions to God can also bring about a successful day or journey (Proverbs 16:3). Getting in the habit of speaking gratitude and having intentional thinking, will bring mental clarity to what you need to do. Once you do this, your mind, body, and spirit will align with those thoughts, and you will be able to visualize all the possibilities that lie ahead.

As you work to develop this habit, at first like any other, you may have to schedule this time to make sure it happens, but soon after you commit to this practice consistently, it will become your nature. It will be important to guard this time, because if you don't many things will take its place. When other things are more important than meditating on God's word, spending time in his presence and seeking wisdom and guidance, time spent thinking forward, you may find yourself in reaction mode. Reacting to what happens throughout your day, as opposed to being proactive and preparing your mind, body and spirit on how to walk into your day, is more productive.

To focus our minds on meditating on his word, we can be successful in what we do. Sometimes, you may have to take a moment, step back, inhale, exhale and say, "I will control how I respond to this, this will not control me". I am not saying this is a "fix it" to all problems and tough times that come your way, but it is a way to proactively train your mind and you choose how you will respond to hardships and how you show up. When my father passed away a couple of years ago, I had to make the choice to adapt and adjust to my grief and lean into it. But I have to tell you that as I look back on that time, I realize the grace of God is what allowed me to keep moving forward in my calling. There will be times you will just have to lean in, and deal with the issue at hand as you see fit and allow the grace of God to help you through.

You may find that taking this time daily to be grateful can condition your mind to focus when it seems all hope is lost. You will be more focused on God's plan for your life and not your own. As you include gratitude in your day, it places emphasis on the things you can control. You can control your thought process, and the idea is to adjust, keep moving, and keep trusting in God.

Some days when you feel overwhelmed, remember one thing you can control, is being grateful. You may have forgotten to do something. You may have made mistakes, or been hurt or betrayed by someone, but in the midst of the situation, focus on what you can control. This can ground your thoughts and emotions in the moment, so you don't get stuck or spiral downward. I spent some time studying the book of Joshua and as I read a particular passage, it jumped off the page to me and into my heart. It helped me to realize what I am responsible for and what God promises to do as a result of my obedience. In chapter one verse 8 of Joshua, God is very clear on how to be successful, and he says to the children of Israel, "this book of instruction must not depart from your mouth; you are to meditate on it day and night so that you may carefully observe everything written in it. *For then* you will prosper and succeed in whatever you do" (my emphasis). So, if this was good enough for the children of Israel on their journey to the promised land, it certainly is good enough for me. Developing a habit of making room for gratefulness, is being intentional about your thoughts and might I suggest to you, this can lead you to success of loving yourself well and teaching others how to love you well.

Scriptures to meditate on and questions to ponder:

Colossians 2:10, 1 John 4:7-11, 1 Thessalonians 5:18, 2 Corinthian 12:9

1. Knowing God is to know love. How have you experienced God's love in your life?
2. What are three things you are grateful for today?
3. How can knowing that God's grace is sufficient help you to love yourself well?

Chapter 2
WHOLENESS: LIVING A BALANCED LIFE: MIND, BODY, & SPIRIT

Mind

"On the glorious splendor of Your majesty and on Your wonderful works, I will meditate." Psalms 145:5

Quiet reflection and gratitude are important in living a purposeful life, and you will find that if you do not schedule this time for yourself daily, it is likely it will not happen. So be intentional. There are many times in the word of God where prophets were told to sleep, or to go to a certain destination and rest, under a tree, and etc. Even Jesus took time and went away and the bible says to be with the Father and pray (Luke 5:16). God while creating the world, creatures, and mankind, he rested (Genesis 1). It is important for your mind, body, and spirit to rest well in order for your mental, emotional, and physical attributes to operate the way they were created to. God designed the human body to require rest so that during rest, the body can heal and recover. Even small breaks throughout the day can be beneficial and good for you. This leads to one way you can obtain the necessary rest your mind needs in order to flourish: Biblical meditation.

Biblical meditation is encouraged by God, so we should not shy away from this design to rest and reflect on the goodness of God. As stated before, in Joshua 1:8, God instructed the children of Israel to meditate on the book of instructions day and night. Meditating daily will be a helpful habit as you walk in purpose. You will need moments of clarity that can only come from meditation. Meditation can guard your mind from unnecessary thoughts and cares of the world. If you grasp this idea you will also find that meditating daily can improve your mind, body, and spirit. It can improve and grow you as you move forward. Taking control of what comes in and what flows out of your mind through meditation, will present a sense of clarity you may never have experienced before. Biblical meditation can bring you a sense of comfort and peace, which will be beneficial on your journey of purpose.

It takes great courage and humility to move forward into what God is calling you to, which is your purpose. We are used to moving in the same circles and doing the same things. I have even had clients tell me they are creatures of habit. Biblical meditation may be something new and even strange to you. You must get accustomed to pouring back into your empty vessel, daily. You are taking care of everyone and everything and leaving the crumbs for yourself. It is simple and you choose the time of day that works best for you, but you must allow the Holy Spirit to pour into you what is needed for you to continue to walk in purpose.

Meditating on scriptures of God's divine nature is simple. Sometimes we make things so complicated that we get lost in what and not why it is necessary. Simply meditating on the word of God or pondering a spiritual principal, takes a moment without thinking of anything else. Get some place where you are less likely to be distracted, put your phone on silent, and think on a scripture. As you are pondering the biblical principles, ask yourself some questions. Your questions will be different every time, but they will provoke deep thinking. Try these; How can I apply this passage to my life? Or, God, what are you speaking to me through this passage? God what is your main principle here that I need to understand?

This is a funny story; my husband and I have six children and each one of them is different and are intellectual thinkers in their own way. If you have children, you will probably agree with me that children can ask some really hard questions, that will cause you to have to ponder for a moment in order to arrive at an answer and then communicate it in a way a child can understand. One instance I remember very vividly. My youngest son, Daniel, as a toddler would ask some deep questions for a child his age. One day he was probably about five years old, and asked, how many miles does it take to get to heaven? He was and still is a deep thinker. Of course, I know, and you know, there are no miles to heaven, but just the thought of him equating distance to heaven, to me was astonishing because he was so young at the time. He was pondering based on some information either we had given him, or he learned at church about heaven and was meditating on it. I had no idea how to answer that question, but I pondered it for a moment, and my answer must have been satisfactory because he went on about his way. To ponder a passage, ask God questions, and invite the Holy Spirit to help you. You were created for a purpose and in the image of God. Although our thoughts are not his thoughts and our ways are not his ways (Isaiah 55:9), we are made to be able to create and imagine. Children do this very well, so be childlike again. Use this technique to ponder and meditate on the word of God. Biblical meditation is not to quiet your mind and think of nothing, but it is to ponder the works of an Almighty God, and this will lead you to a closer relationship with God.

Okay, so let's take a step back for context. Genesis 1:1-2 tells us "In the beginning God created the heavens and the earth. And the earth was a formless and desolate emptiness, and darkness was over the surface of the deep and the Spirit of God was hovering over the surface of the waters", some translations say, "in his likeness". God is the Creator, because he made something out of nothing, and we were made in his image, that goes to say we are also creative. Being a creative being, means you have the ability to create something with your mind, hands, even with your imagination that has never been done before. This is a big idea, but it's true and partnering with God, during meditation, can lead you to your creative side.

Scripture also tells us in Ephesians 3:20-21, *that God can do anything that we can even imagine.* I love this, he gently works with us in partnership. If you take time to think about how you are in collaboration with the Almighty God who spoke the world and everything in it to existence, and it was, you will find how amazingly things flow into place. Be strong and courageous to go places you've never been, or do things you've never done, and yes, even imagining things and bringing them to life. You can't know that something will work if you don't try it. So don't hold back, keep moving, jump in with both feet and keep growing. Biblical meditation allows you the time to get to know the Almighty God, his nature, and his attributes. Biblical meditation is not to dumb down your mind, but to walk in partnership with God so you can fulfill your purpose on this earth.

Meditating, and spending quiet time to think on good things, can set your mood for the day, or can realign your heart in the middle of the day, or even settle your spirit before you go to bed at night.

Body

"Or do you not know that your body is a temple of the Holy Spirit within you, whom you have from God, and that you are not your own?" 1 Corinthians 6:19

When you hear the word wellness or read it somewhere, it usually has something to do with dieting, excessively exercising or fitness and mental health. Okay, maybe not exercising that much. I need you to know this is coming from someone who doesn't necessarily like working out, but I do it because it's good for my body, mind, & spirit. Because I am not a fan of working out and I do it because I must keep active, I make sure I am mindful of the fuel I put into my body. Hopefully this will be a good balance and I will give my body what it needs to operate at its highest potential.

When you show up, it is important to show up feeling your best and looking your best. Taking care of your body is another way to love yourself. For you to feel your best, you want to make sure you are making wise choices. Everyone is different in terms of what your physical needs are and what your limitations are, and only you know that. The most important thing for you to take away from this section is that if you are not taking the best care of yourself, by what you are putting into your body, it's time for you to start doing so. I'm not talking about following every diet and workout trend out there, because not everything will work for everyone. I am simply saying, to understand your body and be mindful that when you feel good and look good, you act good. Acting good translates into a high level of confidence and courage that will help you show up ready to let your light shine and if you let your light shine, let God be glorified! It's important to understand that "you have been bought for a price: therefore, glorify God in your body" (1 Corinthians 6:20). What is also important to know is that, in order to get your spirit and your mind right, you have to get your body right, first. For the bible says, the spiritual is not first but the natural; then the spiritual" (1 Corinthians 15:46).

Spirit

"But I say, walk by the Spirit, and you will not carry out the desire of the flesh."

Galatians 5:16

In chapter 1, we discussed the importance of having positive conversations with yourself and others. Feeding your spirit is very important for your body and mind to work in concurrence. It is quite simple because everything you take in has the potential to either lift your spirit or weigh you down. You make the choice. Sometimes that can look like the community that you've become a part of or individuals who you allow to speak into your life.

Take ownership and, take into consideration what you are allowing into your spirit. Be very aware. Negativity can brew in your mind and your being for a while, without you being aware and then you find yourself in the same place you were this time last year, with no growth or progression, upset, bitter, and blaming others for you being stuck.

I learned later in ministry, what you feed grows and what you starve dies; which means the more of what you give your spirit will continue to grow. So, if you are feeding bitterness, anger, or resentment, then guess what, bitterness, anger and resentment will grow. But if you take time to manage your thoughts daily, and when negative thoughts come in, how quickly you respond to them will determine whether that seed grows or dies. In other words, if you don't check those thoughts, they will settle in your spirit.

Negative thoughts that go unchecked can foster an environment that can cause you to get stuck. That is the last thing you want while on this journey. It is important to develop muscle memory that combats negative thoughts and limiting beliefs. Those of you who are familiar with this term "muscle memory" understand that if you do something long enough, your mind and body develops a memory pattern which will respond automatically in that way. So, as you are faced with limiting beliefs and negative thoughts, because you have taken the time to pour into your spirit things that are healthy, true, honorable, and good, your unconscious mind will generate opposition to these thoughts, but with intentional work. You are then able to keep moving forward. As your thoughts are redirected, your behaviors will then be redirected. The idea here is that you don't waste good energy on negative thoughts.

Creating an internal atmosphere within your spirit of positivity to accomplish your goals while on this journey, will take work. What you put into your spirit plays a big role in how you show up and complete the work you need to do. Being intentional about how you feed these areas (mind, body, spirit) will determine how quickly you adjust and redirect. If either of these areas are weak, it will affect the other, so make sure you are creating a necessary balance between the three and that's why meditating day and night are important principles.

Scriptures to meditate on and questions to ponder:

Isaiah 55:8-11, Ecclesiastes 5:1-4, Colossians 3:2-10

1. How can biblical meditation play a role in you managing your mind, body, and spirit?
2. Reflecting on your thought journey, what do you find yourself giving more attention to in your life, what are you feeding?
3. As you meditate on God's word in the scriptures above, what are some principles you will need to apply to your life?

Chapter 3
WALK IN PURPOSE SACRIFICIALLY

"Therefore I urge you, brothers and sisters, by the mercies of God, to present your bodies as a living and holy sacrifice, acceptable to God, which is your spiritual service of worship" Romans 12:1

You may be in a position where you like what you do, and you enjoy everything about it. You probably are good at what you do and there must be some benefit for being where you are, otherwise, you wouldn't be there. If this is the case, then let's talk about how you stay where you are and while you are there, how you create a space where you are pleasing God and serving people. Once you have the job or career, how do you keep it? You want to always find yourself in a space that encourages growth, learning, and development, and this should always be on your mind. Know that anything that has to do with your purpose, will have to do with service. Pleasing God and serving others is why we are walking in purpose. So, how do you do that sacrificially and not hating what you get to do?

There are four things to remember as you learn to please God and serve sacrificially.

1)Walk in true worship, 2) Love those you serve, 3) Do not avenge yourself, and 4) Love some more.

Walk in True Worship

"God is spirit, and those who worship Him must worship in spirit and truth." John 4:24

Walking in true worship, literally means you position yourself for worship while you work, so to speak. Although you are walking in purpose, you sacrifice greatly. The sacrifice will be time, rest, money/resources, talents, and other areas, which hopefully you practice balance to ensure your loved ones do not pay the price for your sacrifices. There will be times as you are serving that you will have to be reminded to rest. You will grow accustomed to flowing in your gifts and your champions around you will let you know when you need to take a break. Don't feel guilty or ashamed, because you are human, and rest is required. You want to make sure you set yourself apart from others, renew your mind (Romans 12:2) and be so self-aware that you know when rest is needed and allow that for the people you are serving. Rest brings clarity and hopefully you will find the ability to hear clear instructions from the Father. Worship in true humility which in turn will be a sweet aroma to please God.

Love

"Love must be free of hypocrisy. Detest what is evil; cling to what is good. Be devoted to one another in brotherly love; give preference to one another in honor"

Romans 12:9-10

We are reminded in this passage of scripture, that love is an action word. In order to walk in purpose, you will have to be free to love in such a way, that as you serve others, you are not looking for anything in return. The bible uses words like; devoted, freedom, honor, serving, contribution, hospitality in how we are to demonstrate love by serving others. Serving others can be sacrificial if you have committed your life to walking in purpose. You are encouraged to give without expecting anything in return, because your purpose was placed inside of you by the Creator God with a plan in mind.

Do Not Avenge Yourself

"Never take your own revenge, beloved, but leave room for the wrath of God, for it is written: "Vengeance is mine, I will repay," says the Lord." Romans 12:19

As you are walking in purpose, you will find there will be times, people will be against you. They may slander your name and lie on you. It is not our business what others say about us. We have a God given gift to walk in dominion while on this earth, and you don't want to waste time thinking or reflecting on those who are intimidated by you. You must stay focused on what God has called you to do and take pleasure in knowing He's got your back. Jesus Christ, the son of God, even showed us an example of this while on the cross (Luke 23:34). He being God in human form, could have at any point taken vengeance out on the ones who hung him there. But he cried out to the Father to forgive them. When you think about how you have been hurt and what has been said about you, don't think long but ask the Father to forgive and you move on, because you have work to do. Life's too short to marinate on things and waste time and energy on what someone has done to you. This doesn't mean they will not go unpunished because the word also says, "for whatever a person sows, this he will also reap" (Galatians 6:7). It is not up to us to make them pay, so don't make that your business. Stand on God's business and keep moving forward.

Love Some More

"Love is patient, love is kind, it is not jealous; love does not brag, it is not arrogant."

1 Corinthians 13:4

There are times, Lord help me, when I am helping and serving and it seems like everything I do, seems to fall on deaf ears and there is no impact. Once, I thought about this and I realized that in my love, I am expecting something in return and that is not God's design for us. Because I am not perfect and desire patience from others, I have to be patient and kind when serving. No matter what, it is not an option, it actually is a command. When I think about it this way, my heart opens, and I am able to love deeply. I recognize that in order for me to love well, I must love without accepting anything in return, except to love. We must love our neighbor as ourselves (Romans 13:8-9). Sometimes it is hard to fathom, loving just to love, but when you feel the love of God, you know love and He can help you love in this way. His love is perfected in us (1 John 4:12).

Focus On Pleasing God

"Do nothing from selfishness or empty conceit, but with humility consider one another as more important than yourselves;"
Philippians 2:3

Have you ever been in the company of someone, or persons and you could tell they didn't really care about the people in the group, they were only concerned about what they would get out of the deal? You can tell right off the bat when this is the case. People can tell when you're not authentic or genuine and if you remember how this feels when you are in the company of these individuals, it can make you feel unimportant or devalued. The bible tells us, "do not merely lookout for your own personal interests, but also for the interests of others" Philippians 2:4.

When walking in purpose, keep your focus pleasing God. Shift your mindset to what the things are that you love doing that are a part of your job, and how you can do it in such a way that you are grateful every day because of what you get to do for others.

When getting clear on your purpose, see how you operate in your current role and use your gifts and passions in a creative way. Take a moment and think about what it is you are currently doing, if you enjoy doing it, the way you continue to enjoy doing it is by taking the focus off of you. Serving others can bring you great joy and satisfaction. Your gift has been placed inside of you to add value to others. If you place the focus on others, you will begin to feel as though it is not a job and Monday mornings will be greatly anticipated. Here's a few ways you can keep your focus on pleasing God and serving others: 1. Be humble, 2. Read God's word for instructions, 3. Follow God's precepts, and 4. Acknowledge the value others bring to the table.

Practice Humility

"The reward of humility and the fear of the Lord are riches, honor, and life."

Proverbs 22:4

Another way you can find purpose in what you do is by staying humble. Now, let's get this straight. To be humble does not mean you are weak! The definition of the word humility is to have a modest or low view of one's own importance (New Oxford American Dictionary). This does not mean that you will disrespect yourself or put yourself down in a negative way to make someone else feel better about themselves. No, this means you are in great control when you are moderate and unassuming in how you honor or treat others.

In humility, there is a great deal of respect for others. You are very much aware of who you are and the value you add. You are confident in God's design of you, and you celebrate where others are. You are not intimidated by them because you understand, we all bring a special spice to the table to work in conjunction with each other. When someone is humble, they are always willing to serve and help others excel, while they are confidently showing up, themselves. There is a great deal of wisdom that comes with humility. The bible tells us "When pride comes, then comes dishonor; but with the humble there is wisdom" Proverbs 11:2.

Serving others is a great form of humility for a great leader who knows themselves and is comfortable with who they are. There are three ways to practice humility to find purpose in what you do, so you can be great! Beginning with these items, will pave the way for you in your current role or the role you are transitioning into, to stand out amongst the crowd as a leader (Luke 1:11). 1. Acknowledge the people that help you achieve – Letting others know how much you appreciate their help. Don't let it go unnoticed. 2. Be teachable – showing up as someone who is teachable, resembles a great team player. 3. Celebrate milestones – it is not only important to celebrate your milestones, but celebrating others' is an awesome way to show humility.

Scriptures to meditate on and questions to ponder:

Romans 12:9-18, James 4:6-7, John 13:34-35

1. How has someone loved you well and what did it look like?
2. How do you feel when the alarm clock wakes you in the morning to go to work? 3. What are your thoughts about leading with humility?

Chapter 4
DISCOVER YOUR PURPOSE

"I pray that the eyes of your heart may be enlightened, so that you will know what is the hope of His calling..." Ephesians 1:18

You might find this chapter the most difficult if you are not yet clear on your purpose, but it will take you being intentional about what you are doing, what you are reading, where you are going and who you are talking to. Sometimes, we can make it so difficult to figure this out, but it is quite simple. A great place to start is by pressing into the word of God which is our manual.

I remember sitting down and calculating my life journey when I went off to college with the high hopes of becoming a judge. I remember being so excited about that and feeling even accomplished in my thoughts in terms of what I wanted to do when I grew up. Going into my sophomore year in college, I began making some phone calls to see if I could get an internship for the summer at the courthouse in my hometown. I talked to the District Attorney's Office about hiring me as an intern for the summer. I communicated what I wanted and how it would benefit me in my education and how they would play an integral role. That summer is when I learned being a lawyer and then a judge was NOT what I wanted to do. I was able to have conversations with Assistant District Attorney, paralegals, and administrators in the office and asked key questions that could help me figure it out. What education would look like. What skills were needed and if I even wanted to pursue this career. I am thankful for that time in my life and my desire to seek wisdom and guidance. That was one time of many, when I implemented the importance to seek wise counsel, and this is what you will need to do. Others can sometimes help you see your purpose, so wise counsel is necessary. The bible tells us in Proverbs chapter 15 and verse 22, that "Without consultation, plans are frustrated, but with many counselors they succeed." If you are not in the habit of asking for help, you are going to need to get there in order to be successful. If you are already operating in your purpose, this chapter will help you clarify the journey and teach you how to adjust and adapt when necessary. Seeking wise counsel and always learning, will be important in walking in purpose.

This is truly a journey, and you will feel like it is mostly trial and error, or should I say, trial and trial. There is no error because you are researching and learning about yourself in terms of what next steps need to look like. You are utilizing resources that will help to make your way clear. If you stay the course, put the work in and keep moving, you will get clearer with every step. This is about finding your "sweet spot". By doing this, you will learn to use your voice to tell people what you need. This will not happen overnight, and it will take work on your part. Implementation is one step in creating and building, and you will want to put action to your imagination, thoughts, and ideas. Sometimes you will feel like nothing is happening but all you are doing is work, work, work. But don't be discouraged, stay the course, and keep your focus on walking out your purpose!

Press In

"So let's learn, let's press on to know the LORD" Hosea 6:3

When thinking about your interests and passions, what do you flow in and when you're doing it do you lose track of time? What would you do any day of the week without getting paid? Or better yet, what do you find yourself doing that is beneficial for others in some way and you're not currently getting paid to do it?

These are questions you should take time to answer and write them down. When I began my journey of discovering my purpose, I remember looking back as far as my first job, working at a fast-food restaurant. I remember the first and last week I spent there; I knew it wasn't for me. So, the journey began, and I wanted to know what was next for me. Not until I was in corporate America did I realize I had a gift of encouraging and inspiring people to be their very best self. I was able to establish strong sales teams that would work hard in accomplishing goals. I didn't know that Coaching was even a thing, but I was very satisfied in managing my team in such a way that they knew I cared about them as individuals, not just producers. I knew working with a team to help each of them individually was something I wanted to do, and that began to cultivate a love of exhortation in me. So, I pressed in. I pressed in to help and encourage each person on my team to be their very best selves regardless of sales production. I pressed toward the mark and applied biblical principles by considering others as more important (Philippians 2:3).

Discovering your purpose takes time and effort. It takes a pressing mentality, that only one can have who is determined to walk in what God has predestined for them. To be very honest with you, going to college and getting a formal education is not necessarily something you must do. No one ever says anything about finding something you flow in to determine what your vocation should be. The importance is placed on finding a good, paying job and going to school and getting a degree. As if to say, this is the only way to experience success. I believe in education as a matter of fact, I have two degrees of my own that I worked very hard for. But what I am saying is a formal education may not be for you. Success is not determined by how much money you make, how many degrees you have, or even the position you hold. Success is determined by the individual who has a keen perspective on their life's purpose and the ability to search for that thing that will please God and add value to others. Aligning your thoughts of success with God's will get you where you need to be, and you will be satisfied. King Solomon was said to have been the wisest leader and king who ever lived (1 Kings 4:30). He tells us in Proverbs 9:10 that "the fear of the Lord is the beginning of wisdom, and the knowledge of the Holy One is understanding". Starting here will bring you great success and as long as you aren't seeking success in society's view, you will do well.

Hobby or Purpose

"And we know that God causes all things to work together for good to those who love God, to those who are called according to His purpose." Romans 8:28

A question I get asked often is "How do I know this is not just a hobby or interest? This is a great question, because it shows that you are truly wanting to dive in and do what you were divinely purposed to do. Understanding what you are purposed for and what you enjoy doing, can be very difficult to distinguish between. You can find yourself trying to operate in something that you only like to do but it is in no way serving others. What do I mean by this? Your purpose was created inside of you at the moment of conception (Ephesians 1:11), and it was created for something good. You are given this ability, this passion and love for something that provides growth and ways to enhance the common good of humanity, to fulfill God's will for the earth. Generally, hobbies, or interests are things you like to do for your personal release or feeling. Hobbies or interests are things done that can benefit you in terms of self-care if it is something that helps to energize you. Your purpose can bring you fulfillment, but it will always be beneficial to someone else, not just yourself.

When looking to discover your purpose, coaches will look at the things you enjoy doing, but we help you become clear on how or if you can operate in a particular role in order to benefit others while growing yourself. The things you enjoy doing will most likely be incorporated in your purpose. For example, I love helping people and this could look differently depending on the environment or how I am serving. It is important to look at what it is you like to do, when you do it, how are you feeling, how are you growing and how it makes you feel when you are helping others in this area. The people you trust and who love and care about you can sometimes help you in this area because they will observe you flowing in your gifting and can put a name to it. Try asking someone close to you what is something you flow in. They will not always be right on target in terms of your purpose, but they can get you looking in a direction that can help you start and maybe open some doors or opportunities for you to try something you really enjoy doing. Your champions can be beneficial for you to help you walk in your purpose.

Here's another example, something I really enjoyed doing and that made me feel good about myself, was cheerleading. Yes, I said cheerleading, but I am not trying to jump around in a short skirt for a sports team now. I am better at cheering you on in what it is you are trying to accomplish. So, I put cheerleading to the side and my vocation sounds the same but is different. What I got out of cheering was the fun, smiles, laughter, and energy. Now I use those same things in coaching and training, today. This is how I used what I loved to do to help guide me towards my purpose.

Hobbies are made to energize you; purpose is to please God and serve others! I can't say that enough.

Do I Need to Go to School

"Many plans are in a person's heart, but the advice of the LORD will stand."

Proverbs 19:21

Your gift is a part of your being and your complete make up. You must believe you were created with your purpose in mind. You have everything you need to operate within purpose. However, the society we live in, may dictate the educational level you must have in order to operate in a particular area. This is not always the case, but it can be if you feel called to teaching. Our society says you must have advanced degrees in order to operate in this area of purpose. So, you will need to look at what it is you want to do based on what it is you enjoy doing and once you've identified how you can do your purpose as a vocation, you next want to begin the educational journey that will go along with it.

As a coach, I love pointing clients to resources where they can investigate skill sets, career titles and education necessary. There are many resources out there that will help you look at specific professions and determine if they are right for you. I suggest you think about your skill set, education, love, and passion and determine how this lines up with a specific vocation. When I learned Coaching was a thing, I was already doing it, but I wanted to know more. I wanted to get better at it so I could help thousands of people. Some things you can pursue without having additional degrees or certifications, and coaching is one of them. But there are certifications out there for being a life coach or life strategist, and it is completely up to you to determine if you want to go that route. One of my favorite scriptures is, "commit your works to the Lord, and your plans will be established" Proverbs 16:3. Therefore, if you feel the need to get further education, commit to it and commit it to God and he will make you successful.

You want to make sure you do your due diligence to insure you don't spend anyunnecessary money to get started. You always want to make sure the investment you are making is one that will benefit you and the people you serve. Sometimes that is experience alone, so while you are searching, search well and utilize people who are already in the industry to help you. Find someone who does what you want to do and ask them if you can take them to lunch or for coffee. You can learn a lot by finding a mentor, adviser or coach. Your experience doesn't always have to come in the form of an educational degree. Therefore, it is very important that you do your homework, pray and ask God for direction.

If what you want to do is so specific that not many people know what it is or how it can serve others or even that it is a profession, you must become an expert in that area. You must find individuals you can help in this way and help others see the need for what it is you do. You want to find the solution to a problem and help others solve it. In this case, it is still vitally important to find someone who does what you want to do or is very closely related to what you want to do and have a sit down with them. When you do this, you will want to rate their credibility based on their experience and what they have been able to accomplish. Again, this takes work and time which will generate growth and value in you and others.

Scriptures to meditate on and questions to ponder:

Philippians 3:12-15, Philippians 4:9, 1 Corinthians 15:10

1. What is something you have dreamed of doing for years?
2. What can you press into that could help you discover your purpose?
3. How can you learn more about what you feel most passionate about?

Chapter 5
APPLICATION

"Now for this very reason also, applying all diligence, in your faith supply moral excellence, and in your moral excellence, knowledge," 2 Peter 1:5

Okay, so hopefully you have learned some things about yourself, how to love yourself and others well, balance your mind, body, and spirit, and discovering your purpose. You are understanding the importance of beginning to schedule time for reflection and deep introspection to be able to know where you are, where you want to go, and how to bridge the gap, with divine instruction. These are all tools for your toolbox to help you continue to move forward and to coach yourself through the different phases or seasons of life. I know you have heard that old saying "Knowledge is power". That is only correct if you apply the knowledge you gain, then it can become powerful! Applying the knowledge, wisdom, experiences you have gained, will be proven to act as motion. Knowledge in motion is what you want, so let's begin to condition your mind to put your knowledge to action. The idea here is to "apply your heart to discipline, and your ears to words of knowledge" (Proverbs 23:12). Stay diligent and focused on this phase to progress into purpose.

Application is very important to bring forth your purpose in such a way that as you move forward in your purpose, others will glean knowledge and wisdom from you to help them move forward. Remember, your purpose is to serve others. Some people spend much of their life learning and getting knowledge, and getting more knowledge and more, but they never stop to implement or apply the knowledge they've learned. What a waste. Real life situations need your knowledge applied to them so you can continue to grow and be empowered to continue to walk out your purpose. Not for the sake of business or just making money, but it is all about accomplishing your life goals and purpose so others can benefit from what you do. Commitment is necessary, in the application stage, otherwise, you are just dreaming.

Create

"For we are His workmanship, created in Christ Jesus for good works, which God prepared beforehand so that we would walk in them." Ephesians 2:10

You've imagined and dreamed, now it's time to create. In Genesis, chapter one, we learn how and what God created and in all of his creation, he also created you and I in his image. We are image bearers of the one who created us. So, if He is creative and created something out of nothing (Gen 1:1-2), believe you also bear this quality. Many studies have been done that tell us how long it takes to form a habit. I've read, twenty-one days or even thirty days doing something consistently helps to form habits. We do know for sure it takes repetition of doing something for a long time, creating mind habits and parts of our thought processes. So, let's go with thirty days, think of something you have been doing for let's say some years, something that may not be beneficial for you. Now think about something you can do to replace that habit that will benefit you in your purpose. Write it down and make it a part of your daily walk journey. I say daily walk journey, because daily you will need to repeat this action in order to have a mind shift take place, so it becomes a part of who you are and what you do. It will need to be a transformation of your mind (Romans 12:2) that will bring the fruit of intentionality for change. What sacrifices will you have to make? What difficult conversations will you have and what people will you possibly need to cut out of your life or at least decrease the amount of time you spend with them.

Did you know that God set and established boundaries all throughout scripture (Exodus 23:32). This is fascinating, because most of the time when I encourage individuals to establish boundaries, they feel as if they are doing something bad or something hurtful, in some way. I hope that freed someone today. Boundaries are set to ensure you stay within the realm of pleasing God and serving others. Matthew 7:16 says, "you will know them by their fruits. Grapes are not gathered from thorn bushes, nor figs from thistles, are they?" Boundaries are good.

Create your plan by first taking time to write out exactly what it is you are wanting to accomplish and why. Make this a habit of writing your goals down. You are going to want to research potential problems you can solve, acquire your specific skills, and begin to craft your ideas and put them to action. Create your plan and create opportunities to activate them.

Communicate

"Let no unwholesome word come out of your mouth, but if there is any good word for edification according to the need of the moment, say that, so that it will give grace to those who hear." Ephesians 4:29

In Genesis 1, God imagined, created, and spoke. If you are not used to speaking out, you will have to commit to being uncomfortable. Start with having a conversation with someone and let them know what your plans are or what it is you would like to do and ask them for help. Give people the opportunity to work with you or let you know if they have some boundaries in place that might limit them in some way, but at least, give others the chance to guide you. Let others know what you are doing and how you can help them solve a problem. We talked about writing things down, do this so you become familiar with what you are doing and practice saying it over and over, so it becomes second nature to you and believable to others. Use your voice to tell others how you want to help them and what problems you are able to solve. You have to speak what you have imagined in order to go to the next step of fulfilling your purpose. If you don't speak it, then again, it is just a dream with now application.

One way you can use your voice to progress into purpose is by conducting informational interviews with individuals who can pour into you. This journey is not designed for you to take alone. There are people in your community and within your circles who remember what it was like when they were seeking guidance and clarity. An information interview is you setting up a phone call or in person visit with someone who does what you are interested in doing. Take a list of questions to ask them. This will give you knowledge on a role, profession, industry, or career from someone who has a unique perspective. Having that one-on-one insight can lead you in such a way that it can possibly offer opportunities just by using your voice.

There are opportunities out there that will give you direct connection and interaction in the role you are interested in like apprenticeships or internships if that's something you would like to do. Usually when people hear these words, apprenticeship, and internship, they think you are supposed to be in school or pursuing some formal education. It is true that these words were designed for the student learner, but I believe, if you are learning whether you are in school or a student of your craft, these opportunities can give you what you need. Don't let that hold you back. Utilize this time to learn as much as you can about what you want to do and apply the knowledge everyday as you walk in your purpose. Practice makes progression and creates muscle memory, so create and work it.

When meeting others to help you grow, alsoutilize webinars, conferences, and seminars on your topic of focus. When communicating and activating your purpose, meet someone over a cup of tea who can be beneficial in helping you walk it out. Remember, you are going to have to be comfortable in being uncomfortable, because you are destined for a great work (Jeremiah 29:11) and unless you are committed to the process, it is going to take you a long time to activate and apply what you have learned and will continue to learn.

Practice

"If you know these things, you are blessed if you do them." John 13:17

How do you begin practicing your plan? You take a step and then another. Take one step at a time and move toward your purpose. Move towards being successful in what you get to do every day. My mom says, "you have to do what you have to do in order to do what you want to do", so with this in mind, take the step. Even when you feel you are not completely ready, still take the step. No one is needing you to be perfect, but they are looking for you to move. There is a call on your life (Romans 8:30), and it is time to stop making excuses as to why you can't. God is a gracious God (Ephesians 2:8). He did not create you with a purpose and then not give you what you need to fulfill it (2 Timothy 3:17).

Search for opportunities in the role you are transitioning to and step into them. Volunteer with organizations, you will be helping them and yourself. Serving is the way to walk out your purpose and to make your dreams come true. This will give you the opportunity to network and build your list of resources because as you walk out your purpose, you will need others along the way.

Remember, be willing to be comfortable in being uncomfortable!

Scriptures to meditate on and questions to ponder:

Genesis 1:1-31, 2 Peter 1:3-10, 2 Timothy 3:16-17

1. Take some time to write down some habits you think you have that need to be removed from your daily journey and next to them some new habits that can replace the old ones.
2. Think about what it is you want to do. As you think about that, write down what it will take for you to begin walking it out.
3. What sacrifices will you have to make to do it?

Chapter 6
BECOME A BETTER COMMUNICATOR

"Your speech must always be with grace, as though seasoned with salt, so that you will know how you should respond to each person."
Colossians 4:6

You must understand that communication is important for your daily function, relationships, and activities. I think it's safe to say that we must be able to communicate effectively with others for our purpose to be fulfilled. The idea here is that in your communicating, you are delivering your message as clear and concise as possible. You must communicate in a way that you are not misunderstood, with your audience in mind.

You can ask anyone if they feel they are an effective communicator and probably 99% of the time, they will say they are based on how they are used to communicating. Everyone thinks they are an effective communicator until relationships begin to struggle, suffer, or you find yourself not progressing. There is a benefit to learning how to listen and speak in such a way that your message is received in the manner it is intended and for the audience it is intended for. You want to make sure the individuals who should be hearing your message are the ones you are communicating with, otherwise, you can be wasting your time and talents. Proverbs 18:13 says, "One who gives an answer before he hears, it is foolishness and shame to him." Your purpose is to solve a specific problem for a specific group of people. Not everyone needs or will even want to hear your message. Focus on your audience and give them what they want.

A big part of communication is being able to understand from a point of empathy. Always having the individual or your audience in the forefront of your mind in terms of helping them or serving them, can help you deliver your message effectively. Understanding the importance of effectively communicating will enhance your way of helping and serving others. And most importantly, the individuals you are communicating with will feel important and valued when interacting with you. Effectively communicating can add value to others, even a stranger on the street will feel seen and heard, after interacting with you.

Effectively communicating will help to add value to others and enhance your growth. Let's look at a few ideas on how best to improve your communication and why being effective at it matters. You will get an understanding on how to use your voice and when to scale back when necessary. You are going to learn the importance of knowing your audience and why knowing them will improve the way you communicate with them. The art of communicating is one we all can benefit from if we are honest with ourselves. Communicating in such a way where someone feels understood and understands you, shows them you truly hear them. And you don't have to agree with them As humans, we want to be understood, valued, seen, and heard.

Seek First to Understand, Not to Be Understood

"You know this, my beloved brothers and sisters. Now everyone must be quick to hear, slow to speak and slow to anger;" James 1:19

There are times when you have this pressing issue on your heart and you are trying to communicate it to someone of importance, but as the words are leaving your mouth, there is a look of confusion, and you are wondering what is going through the person's head. What are they thinking about, and you ask yourself, am I not being clear, or do they not understand? Even amid these times, you want to try to salvage the conversation so you begin to repeat yourself or raise your voice an octave, to in some way help them to hear you better, but this still doesn't mean they understand you better, just because they can hear you more. It's silly to raise your voice to be understood, but we all do it at some point in our lives.

Try this on for size, when you are communicating with someone, remember you are listening with your eyes, ears, and whole body. Be mindful of what you are doing with your arms, eyes, and facial expression. Are your eyebrows scrunched or raised? Are you leaning into the person or are you looking away at something else that has distracted you? All these things matter in how you communicate and how you are being perceived while you are communicating. A person can tell by your facial expressions and body language if you are really interested and engaged in what they are saying or if you are even taking the time to listen. A practice on how to show someone you are fully engaged is by doing these five things:

1. Don't interrupt.
2. Nod your head and make sounds of agreement.
3. Look directly at the individual, alertly – eye to eye contact is always important.
4. Once they have finished, paraphrase some things to make sure you have heard them correctly.
5. Validate them or what you've heard – you're connecting with the individual on feelings and emotions.

Once you have tried this with a friend or someone, you will see what it feels like to really be intentional about how to listen. This will help you learn how important it will be for someone to be fully engaged. Once you have done this several times, you should begin to feel more comfortable, and you will even begin to teach others how to communicate in this manner with you.

Find Your Voice and Know When to Scale Back

"When I was a child, I used to speak like a child, think like a child, reason like a child; when I became a man, I did away with childish things." 1 Corinthians 13:11

This can be a difficult task and it takes maturity. Be patient with yourself because there will be times when you will not get it right. You may speak up when it's not time and you will have to apologize. There will be times when you should have spoken up and you didn't, and you will need to apologize, as well. Learning this will also help you with knowing how to be humble in how you show up because anytime you must apologize for something you did or did not do, definitely creates a humble spirit. "When pride comes, then comes dishonor; but with the humble there is wisdom" Proverbs 11:2. Humility is not a weakness, but a sign of wisdom and is important in how you communicate.

Many think that if you can speak loudly and project your voice, this is the only way you can show up excellently and get others to listen. Not so, it's about how you listen that can get others attention. How you lead humbly and quietly, but when it's necessary for you to speak up, that is exactly what will be remembered. Those listening will be attentive to your voice because you have shown up humbly and what you've said in those times, proven to be profound and strong (James 3:13).

To hear, you must listen with your whole self. Listening equates to hearing the other person out, not interrupting, paraphrasing what they have said so you and they are sure you heard correctly, and letting your eyes and ears tell the story. When it's time for you to speak because you have listened well, you are able to

articulate yourself in such a way others will feel compelled to hear you. Use your voice when you have facts and not only with your opinion. Use your voice when your facts coincide with your opinions. Use your voice when your purpose is necessary in the room and those involved can benefit from hearing your voice. Know when to scale back and when to speak up.

How to know when to scale back? Think about a time when you have been to some place where you did not feel welcome. Where were you and had you been invited by someone? How did you feel? How did you feel about yourself and how you showed up? Did you feel alone surrounded by tons of people? Now think about you taking a message in that space and if it would be welcomed or received. Would your voice be productive? In order for individuals to learn and grow, they must be able to receive the message being delivered and they have to be able to see a need for the message. You can talk until you are blue in the face, but if you are not being received or if this is not the time for you to speak, the message will go unheard. So, know where you are and who's listening. Determine the space you are in and if it is the appropriate time to speak and be heard. Listen to your inner voice, and let the Holy Spirit guide you and your words. There are times when you are to only listen and not speak. I believe the Holy Spirit can only teach in moments when we are quiet and listening for his voice and our mouth is shut. When it comes to you using your voice, understand that "when there are many words, wrongdoing is unavoidable, but one who restrains his lips is wise" (Proverbs 10:9). Be mindful of when to speak and when it is necessary to listen and observe. There are times during this process, you will want to learn from others, and you can't do that if you are talking too much.

Solve A Problem

"And whoever does not receive you nor listen to your words, as you leave that house or city, shake the dust off your feet." Matthew 10:14

It is very important to know your audience or at least know what they are looking for from you. What is their specific need and why are they here? Be focused on giving the individual(s) what they need and be able to connect with them on their level. No one likes to be listening to someone who is way over their head and is having a problem following. Sometimes you will need to adjust based on the person's feedback. They may say, "I'm having a difficult time following you" and if so, don't take it personal, adjust. The idea is that your message is heard, so you want to be flexible and adapt when necessary.

Do your homework and seek God first (Matthew 6:33), so your message or content is what is needed in the situation. I remember when I was preparing for a diversity training class I was asked to teach. All of the work had been done, outside of the actual in person teaching and training, through an amazing amount of research. I wanted to make sure I would be coming from a level that each person could understand. You want to make sure you know as much about your audience as possible. Ask for these things before going into a room to teach: who would be attending the training, what departments did they work in, were they part time or full time or both, how did each person interact with the entire organization on some level, or did they only work alongside specific groups of people?

It is best not to go into a room where you don't have a handle on the dynamics or know the audience. Show up ready to speak to the audience that is right for your message.

Scriptures to meditate on and questions to ponder:

1 Peter 4:11, Psalms 19:2, Proverbs 1:5

1. When learning to communicate effectively with others, what could be a set back?
2. What do you feel is the most important aspect of effective communication?
3. Describe a time when you found your voice and how did it feel?

Chapter 7
RELATIONSHIPS THAT FLOURISH

"Two are better than one because they have a good return for their labor"

Ecclesiastes 4:9

Relationships are a big part of who we are as humans. We were created to be relational. Everything you do, even those things that are not directly tied to your purpose, requires relationships at some level. So, why not become masters at making them better.

My husband is a great example of this. He often says he is a shy person and does not feel he is in his element when we are in a crowd of people. However, he will also tell you that because of the work he does, he makes himself uncomfortable. He makes himself come out of his shell to meet people and interact with others. I always laugh when he says how shy he is, but in observing him over the years, he sees the importance of not allowing what he feels as a natural tendency to withdraw from people. Step out of your comfort zone to meet and interact with people from all walks of life and this will add richness to your relationships.

Make sure the relationships you establish on your journey are flourishing in such a way that you can always be what you need to be for others, and they are intern being what you need them to be for you. Creating healthy relationships is vital to pursuing your purpose, just as God created woman for man in the garden because "it is not good for man to be alone" (Genesis 2:18). Remember, the energy, efforts, and wealth you put into yourself and those around you, matters, so you want to make sure you aren't wasting anything special, but you are adding value to others.

Communicate from a Place of Love, Kindness, and Care

"Be devoted to one another in brotherly love; give preference to one another in honor."

Romans 12:10

It is important to be conscious of how you are communicating love not only to the ones you love but to everyone. It takes intentionality when you are in a situation that calls for difficult conversations, to initiate the conversation from a place of love. We must be hospitable to one another without complaint (Remember, who you are and what your purpose is to ensure you are communicating from a place of love). The goal should never be to hurt, but to be received correctly and genuinely. Unless the individual feels loved in the conversation, they may not be willing to receive the message you are attempting to deliver. Love, kindness, and care should be felt always even in situations where discipline occurs (Ephesians 4:2). People can tell if you are authentic in how you deliver the message. Think about yourself and when you are listening to someone on any level, you can tell right off the bat if they are being genuine and authentic, in their delivery and you decide if you want to go any further with them.

Communicating from a place of love also causes you to look at where you are and who has poured into your life over the years. What have they contributed and to always remember where you have come from and what God has allowed you to walk through? Think about what good you can use it for and think about the love and compassion God has for you as his son or daughter. I think about his unconditional love for me, and I remember that I am called to love as well (Colossians 3:12). Sometimes we find this difficult to do depending on the situation for different reasons, but at the end of the day, communicating from a place of love, kindness, and care will make you a better communicator and others will seek you out.

What's Your Communication Style

"And how is it that we each hear them in our own language to which we were born?" Acts 2:8

Generally, when communicating with others, we communicate with those we understand best. It has been suggested that there are four styles of communication: Aggressive, Passive, Passive-Aggressive, Assertive. These are the most talked about styles so let's talk about how to identify them and once you do, how to best communicate so your message is understood.

Aggressive style of communication is when someone doesn't have a problem speaking up for themselves, but they can come across rude while doing so. This individual may seem assertive, but they generally don't take into consideration others' opinions. For this individual, it is "their way or the highway". This communication style can damage relationships and self-esteem.

Passive style of communication is the opposite of an aggressive style. This individual does not speak up for themselves. They find it very difficult to speak out against something if they don't agree, they typically will say "it doesn't matter to them" while on the inside, they are beating themselves up because it wasn't what they wanted. This style of communicating can lead to individuals becoming resentful in a relationship.

A passive-aggressive style of communicating is usually done by everyone at some point but is not healthy in terms of what you are wanting to say and how you are wanting to say it. This comes across in a sarcastic manner. This way isn't healthy because the individuals you are in a relationship with never really know what you're honest or truthful about. Someone who communicates passive-aggressively is saying they want their point to be heard but feels that they will be rejected in some way, or their point not accepted. If you are this style communicator, you aren't taking ownership or responsibility on what your thoughts and opinions are, and you are not taking yourself seriously.

An assertive communicator is someone who speaks up for themselves and sometimes others, in a respectful manner. This individual can easily compromise when they feel it is necessary and they can scale back their voice, especially in a situation where others can be impacted. This individual is clear on expectations and can tell someone how they feel, but also can listen to the other person. This individual is mindful of body language, avoids absolutes or exaggerating words, like always or never, and this person also can use "I" statements effectively. This is the healthiest style of communication because all parties leave the conversation intact and heard.

How do you effectively communicate with each of these style communicators? Here are some ways on how to communicate with each of these styles so you can improve and enhance your relationships.

1. Aggressive - it will be important for you to let them get their point across, to remain calm, if possible, give them direct eye contact and make sure you are showing your attentiveness to their needs. This individual will need to know you are listening actively by nodding your head and you have an open body stance. When you respond, paraphrase what you heard, empathize, and acknowledge their opinion or feelings.

2. Passive – take time to really listen to them. For this person, you will sometimes have to listen for the things that are not said. Also, being mindful of your body language is very important and listening with your eyes as well. Paraphrase what you have heard before you assume what they want to say and take the time to completely understand their point of view and acknowledge that you understand. Let this person know they matter, and their opinion matters, and you want to know what they feel. It's important to pay attention to not only your body language, but theirs too, because they may be saying one thing and doing another that contradicts what they truly feel. They will need to feel safe, so it may take some work in helping them grow in communicating more effectively. If it is an important relationship to you, express to them the importance for them to be open and honest.
3. Passive-aggressive – let them know you honestly want to hear their opinion because it matters to you. Discourage them from being sarcastic because it does not help any situation positively. Let them know because the love you have for them, it's important for them to be real with you. They must know that by them being real with you, you are able to trust them completely.

4. Assertive – communicating with an assertive person will help you with communicating with them if you are not an assertive communicator. You can learn from this style of communication and your relationships will be better for it. This style is what you want to strive for.

It is important to be intentional about being an assertive communicator , but even still some of the other styles come out. The idea is that you are mostly operating in the assertive stage. No one is perfect and will always communicate perfectly even if you mostly operate in the assertive communication style. Continue to work at communicating effectively for you and those you are in relationships with. You will flourish and have open, honest, authentic, kind and God honoring relationships.

Quality in Relationships

"But Jesus went up on the mountain, and there He sat with His disciples" John 6:3

    I remember when my husband and I started dating and getting to know each other, we often met after work. Outside of our jobs, we found time to go to the park, or go to dinner on Friday nights. We would meet every Friday afternoon downtown Atlanta and just walk and have so much fun. While we were having dinner or walking in the park or window shopping, we were learning about each other's likes and dislikes. We talked about our future together. We talked about our dreams and goals, how we were raised, our families, and on and on. Be intentional to spend time with your relationships. In order for a relationship to flourish, you must continue to have quality time because you are always growing and changing. If you are always growing and changing, that means there is always something new to learn.

The time you spend together devoted to building a quality relationship, is very important. It takes scheduling and intentionality. Cherish the time you spend with individuals you are getting to know. As I meet with people I have the opportunity to mentor, I give them questions to answer, and we walk out each open-ended question together. My time with them is important and I value that time. When Jesus was teaching the disciples, they would often eat together, walk together to different places and their conversations were rich and intentional (John 6:3).

Establish Healthy Boundaries

"You have established all the boundaries of the earth; You have created summer and winter" Psalms 74:17

All healthy relationships are founded on a few things and some of those things are vulnerability, honesty, and trust. These three components of a healthy relationship will take the relationship a long way. Vulnerability is important because you want to know that this individual understands you from a place where most don't get to see you, and that individual will not cause you any harm. No one wants to be in a relationship where you can't be trusted, and it is shallow in nature. A part of a healthy relationship is being honest, genuine and authentic while you grow. You can trust your visions, goals, dreams, and heart's conversations in a relationship where these attributes are evident. Establishing these things early in a relationship allows for great longevity and growth always towards good things. Trust is a major factor in relationships, and I have worked with so many couples where trust was an issue early and never dealt with. In most cases, the individuals brought lack of trust feelings into a relationship and no matter what, unless they were ready to heal from past hurts, they were not able to completely trust in the current relationship. You owe it to the individuals you are in relationships with, to not take baggage from previous relationships and project your problems from past relationships onto your current ones.

If you are in a relationship now where there is lack of trust, it doesn't mean that this relationship will not work, but what it does mean is that you have some work to do. Know that and be transparent with the individual. Let them know you have issues with trust, honesty, or being vulnerable. Usually, if you have spent quality time with them, they will decide to walk through the journey with you regardless, but remember, you owe it to them to work on yourself. Find a counselor or therapist and put the work in. Invest in yourself to have a relationship that flourishes. It will be worth the investment. It will help you to trust and love yourself so you can begin projecting something positive on the individuals you are in relationships with.

Setting healthy boundaries is necessary for you and the persons you are in relationships with because it allows both of you to grow together and learn from each other. In sharing boundaries, you share respect for one another and trust that you will love each other well. Having healthy boundaries in place is to ensure your uniqueness and wonderfulness that God created you with, remains in tack (Psalms 139:14)

Learn to Laugh at Yourself

"A joyful heart is good medicine, but a broken spirit dries up the bones."

Proverbs 17:22

    Having the mentality that you can do no wrong or having an expectation that you can make no mistakes, is not healthy. That is too much pressure to place on anyone, let alone yourself. There will be times you will do silly things, or you will mess up, don't stay stuck in that place wallowing in your shame. Lift your head up and laugh. There are so many geniuses out there who have made many errors, but they kept going. The people you serve needs to see your authenticity and how you love yourself when things don't go your way

For me, my favorite thing to do after I have trained and coached all day, is to sit down with my husband and watch a silly movie. My husband is a quick thinker and sometimes we will be watching a silly movie or talking with our children about something, and he will have a silly response to something someone has said and the two of us will burst out laughing and our children are looking at us like, "what's funny". And it does my heart good to hear him laugh from that gut place, which in turn makes me laugh. Vice versa, because I am not as quick on my feet, it may take me a little longer to get a joke or to have a quirky response to something, but when I finally get it, we have a good laugh. I enjoy that about myself, and my husband and the laughter is there and, in most times, it's when we can use it the most. I know you have read and heard about what happens physically when we laugh, the good chemicals respond in our bodies. God created everything we need inside of our bodies to respond and give us what we need to keep moving, stay encouraged, happy and full of joy (Psalms 69:32).

Scriptures to meditate on and questions to ponder:

Psalms 126:3, John 13:34, 1 John 3:11, Romans 13:8

1. Describe a time when you jumped to conclusions about a situation with someone you are in a relationship with. Did you start from a place of love, kindness, and care? What is your communication style Why is it important to be honest and transparent in your relationships?

Chapter 8
FROM PROCESSING TO PROGRESSING

"Brothers and sisters, I do not regard myself as having taken hold of it yet; but one thing I do: forgetting what lies behind and reaching forward to what lies ahead,"

Philippians 3:13

Processing is important and necessary. But in order to be effective on this journey, you will need to progress. Make it a good practice of planning your days and weeks out when you are living on purpose, because there is always going to be something that can redirect your focus. You are reading this because you realize it is time to make some adjustments in your life. Even if you are doing what God has called you to do, there are always areas in life that you will need to enhance. Move forward unapologetically in all areas, love, career, relationships and more.

The focus in this chapter is to keep your purpose, goals, strategies, and plans before you so when you are distracted or life throws you a curveball, you know exactly where you are and what needs to be done. This life is too short for you not to be in a place where you are living out your God-given purpose. There is work to be done and people who are waiting on you. Investing in yourself to walk in purpose takes work. It takes forming new habits and disciplines. Yes, there will be times when you won't feel like it. If you are serious about walking in purpose, you will learn there will be times where you need to step back, take a break, reevaluate, and shift gears.

When I began walking out my purpose, there were times I felt frustrated in the process because it seemed as if nothing was happening. I felt drained and overwhelmed but when that happened, I remembered my "why" and it was bigger than me. Or someone would come into my path, which was not by chance, who needed my help. I remember how desperate I once was to walk in what God has for me. Since walking it out, I have always felt like I don't have a lot of time to do it. I felt like I wasted enough time so now that I have clarity and moving with momentum, every moment counts. Every moment counts when adjusting for my business, every moment counts when there is something for me to implement, every moment counts when I need to cut something out of my life. I adjust now quickly because my purpose is at stake and there are people who need what I have. Learn to adjust quickly as you continue to move forward.

Focus

"Devote yourselves to prayer, keeping alert in it with an attitude of thanksgiving;" Colossians 4:2

Clarifying your "why" very early in your process will help you stay on track. It is important to remind yourself what you are all in for and why. It is important for you to look at this often because there will be times you will not feel like adjusting. There will be times you will want to give up. But you won't because your heart won't let you. You will need to adjust, but you won't feel like it because you realize it will take too much energy. You will try to think your way out of it because it may seem scary. You will have conversations with yourself and convince yourself that it will take too much thought, planning or movement, and there is no way you can do something different or new. With this mindset, you will find yourself being stuck in mediocrity and walking away from God's plan for your life.

Here are three things you can do to keep the "main thing the main thing":

1. Write it down (Habakkuk 2:2) and be clear. Be creative, get it printed on a business card or type it up and include some pictures of your goal.
2. Reflect on it (Acts 10:19)
3. Commit your activities to God (Proverbs 16:3)

Having a champion, someone you trust when you feel stuck, you can reach out to and they will help to get you back on track. Sometimes just talking about your goals and dreams will ignite the fire in you to keep progressing. The art of moving when you feel like standing still is an important part of your progression. It is nothing like knowing there were times when you have jumped on the "struggle bus'' but because you have planned for this ride, you know where to get off and what to do to keep moving towards your goal.

Create and Commit to Timelines

"Each person is to remain in that state in which he was called." 1 Corinthians 7:20

Walking out your purpose calls for creativity, clarity, and commitment. You will want to always be mindful of where you are in the process, what your plan is and what your objectives are at any junction of your journey. Blindly walking on this life journey is not a good practice because you can be blindsided at any time. Being blindsided by life can cause you to step away from your goals for an unexpected amount of time, if you're not careful. Rest is necessary. Knowing where you got off and what you were doing when you stepped away, makes it easier for your return. You will be able to jump right back in and continue to move forward. The idea is to keep progressing no matter what.

Create timelines as you progress forward. These timelines that you create, must be realistic based on what it is you are doing. Forward movement will take great work on your part in order to get things moving. Staying close to meeting your timelines will be helpful. Once you get started, keep moving forward and once you are moving forward, momentum will pick up and you are on your way.Be mindful of your time and schedule and make sure you hold the key.

Now it is time to not only create the timelines, but you must commit to following through. As I discussed the importance of knowing your "why", it must be big enough to sustain you. What does that mean? I'm glad you asked. Having a "why" that is big enough to sustain you means, walking in your purpose is usually your walking in something that is bigger than you., This will be an important factor in keeping you moving forward when you want to quit. When you think about it, you understand that there is nothing that can keep you from reaching your goal because God placed it in you (1 Peter 4:10). Commit to your timelines. This is non-negotiable.

Life will hit so hard at times; you must take a step back so you can propel forward with either the same momentum you had when you first started or with even greater eagerness and determination (2 Corinthians 8:11). The definition of flexibility is "the quality of bending easily without breaking" (Oxford Languages). So, when challenges come, and they will, don't break, bend, adapt and keep it moving. Just writing letters on a page means nothing if you are not bringing them together to create the proper story that you and others can read to make it come to life!

One fall evening in the year 2020, I was on my job preparing to facilitate a virtual workshop. I logged on my computer and began chatting with the students, when my phone flashed with my brother's name on it. I thought to myself that I would call him back. Then one minute later, my older brother was calling, which he never calls. I put my computer on mute, and told my boss I needed to take this call. My brother was on the line and began to tell me that dad fell in the bathroom, and he seemed fine, but they were going to take him to the hospital. I said OK and to keep me posted. I went back to my computer and began interacting with the students again. It felt like seconds, and he was calling back with the dreaded news. "Dad is gone!" There was complete silence, I couldn't speak. I was shocked. He took a fall and within fifteen minutes he transitioned into eternity. The family was completely shocked, and mom was devastated, to say the least. Prior to that dreadful day, a few months earlier, I decided to do some consulting on the side and had booked my second group training contract and committed to the date. I remember being so excited and I worked so diligently on the training manual and in preparation for the big day. When my father passed away, what was I to do? Should I cancel or put my grief to the side and continue on. I took the time I needed from work and spent it with my mother and my sisters. When I returned home, work was waiting for me. I returned to work, but my heart was so broken. My dad was one of my biggest supporters and always encouraged me to go with God. I kept my one-on-one coaching sessions, and I went through with my contracted training event. I was completely transparent with attendees. I completed the training, and everyone was pleased with the outcome. I must say, that was the most difficult thing I could have done, besides burying my father. I had to show up because those ladies needed me and maybe in some ways, I needed them that day. God's grace was sufficient for me (2 Corinthians 12:9) that day. I cannot even tell you how I made it through that full day training class. I will never forget how He brought me through that difficult time.

I told myself that if I stopped, I may not finish and that was the last thing I wanted to do. So, I kept moving. I knew exactly where I left off and I kept moving. Without my faith and trust in God to help me through, I don't know if I could have made it. I relied on my champions, and they showed up for me every time I needed them. If I needed to cry, my husband gave me his shoulder. If I needed to talk about how much I missed talking with my dad, he listened. My sisters and I rallied around each other and became the support and the anchor we all needed. I am still missing my dad, but I know he is in heaven and would be so proud of my accomplishments. Most importantly, he would be very proud that I put all "my trust in God and lean not on my own understanding" (Proverbs 3:5-6) through it all.

Choose Your Champions

"And when day came, He called His disciples to Him and chose twelve of them whom He also named as apostles:" Luke 6:13

When walking out your purpose, sometimes it feels like it is something you're doing alone. If you are walking in purpose, there is no way you will be able to accomplish it alone. You will need others and your champions to be there for you. Hopefully, at this time, you have identified your champions, and you are continuing to have conversations with them throughout your journey. They will be there to support you in ways you won't even believe because they want you to succeed.

You have formed a community with these individuals in mind. Your champions are individuals who support what you are doing. They celebrate you and are your sounding board. They will give you constructive feedback when you ask for it and sometimes when you don't. These individuals will encourage you and hold you accountable because they see God's call on your life. They will encourage you to rest when you need to but because they know the importance for you to achieve, they will be your alarm clock when it's time to get up.

Your champions will encourage you when you feel like giving up. I remember a time, thinking, maybe I shouldn't be venturing in this direction. Maybe, I missed God. I called one of my champions, I told her how I was feeling and the frustration I felt, and she immediately began to speak life. She began to remind me who I am and what I was supposed to be doing. You will have times like this and anyone who tells you because you are walking in your purpose, that you won't have times like this, it's a lie. Question your motives, it's okay to do so, but don't question your purpose. Questioning your motives will help you stay on track and will always keep you humble. Assessing where you are and what you are doing helps to keep you on track.

Selecting your champions is important and you must have standards for those in this role. Here are some ideas of what to look for in champions: Godly men and women, individuals who will pray for you and with you, individuals who are connected to you and individuals who you trust to direct you back when you fall off track.

Remember it is not about you, but it is about all the individuals you need to serve. There is good work you are purposed to do (Philippians 1:6) and even if you need to take a step away for a season, do that, but always come back. Set aside quiet time to hear from God for clarity of what next steps need to look like. It may mean getting away in a different location. It may mean getting away so you can refine your goals and tune in to where you are trying to go. It may mean getting by yourself so you can focus on your goals that will move you to purpose.

Don't let anyone or anything move you away from your purpose, for good. People need what you have. It is your responsibility to walk it out, so you are living a life of success. Keep progressing!

Scriptures to meditate on and questions to ponder:

Colossians 4:2-3, 1 Peter 4:8, Isaiah 26:3

1. Describe a time when you felt stuck in completing an important goal or task?
2. Describe some goals you would like to accomplish and create a timeline to make them happen. Be specific with the who, what, when, where, and how.
3. What replenishes you when you want to quit?

Chapter 9
SACRIFICIALLY WALKING IN PURPOSE

"Wealth obtained from nothing dwindles, but one who gathers by labor increases it." Proverbs 13:11

We have discussed the importance of research, enhancing your craft, investing in a Coach or Mentor to help guide you towards achieving your goals and utilizing the manual our Creator made for us in or to follow his design for us to subdue the earth and walk in dominion over what he has created us for. By continuing to do these things, you will establish best practices that will become familiar and a part of your daily pursuit of purpose. Don't try to do what you see others do or implement what others are doing because you feel if it works for someone else, it can work for you.. This is where I messed up, by looking at others and using their recommendations as set in stone for me. I eventually discovered that not everything works for everyone, but it is imperative to shift quickly once you have determined if something is not working for your benefit (1 Corinthians 10:23).

You should use ideas from others only if you feel they are in line with what it is God has called you to do. When something isn't working, step back. Forced outcomes can lead to bad habits formed and bad decisions made. Understand by having some ideas or plans in your toolbox will not always mean you will need everything there in every season, but it will sometimes mean, sifting through and determining what is best for you in your current season. I always say, "don't try to reinvent the wheel" because someone out there has accomplished what it is you are wanting to accomplish, the difference is, that you are unique to your purpose (1 Corinthians 12:27). You should look to make sure you have your own identity and flavor to what it is you are doing. No one wants a copycat. Be your own person and develop your own identity based on your story and what God calls you to do.

Manage Your Time Well

"Let's not become discouraged in doing good, for in due time we will reap, if we do not become weary." Galatians 6:9

You will find it very important to manage your time well. Time management can be key in determining how you will land when you jump. You are going to want to do things that will benefit you in your purpose. Always look for ways to be intentional about your time and how you spend it. Managing your time down to the time you spend connecting with friends or family. Do not be in a situation where you are allowing others to monopolize your time, always be aware of time spent. When you are planning a get together, you can say something like, "Hey girl I would love to have lunch, can you carve out an hour and a half for us to catch up?" This way she is clear on the time you have built in, and she can also plan accordingly. There may be times where you will have to be flexible, but make it a good practice to schedule out your time so you can continue to do the things you have to do.

In terms of managing your time, this includes scheduling selfcare time and time with your loved ones. You want to make sure you aren't putting your priority relationships on hold to walk out your purpose, because often you will need time with your champions to help refresh you. Learn to unplug at the end of the day, so you can carve out time for the three "R's" - rest, relaxation, and relationships. It is important to unplug every day because you are going to need to recharge or reboot. Even a computer needs to reboot at some point so give yourself the time necessary so you can continue to operate on the highest level possible. You will never finish all the work you have to do in a day. There is always going to be some work to do, so there is no need to work all through the midnight hours, unless you have a deadline you are needing to meet. Otherwise, knowing where you left off, you can pick up the next day with fresh eyes and clarity of thought because you have unplugged at a reasonable hour and have allowed your mind, body, and spirit to rest.

Here are some suggestions on how to manage your time well:

1. Get a system on how to keep track of appointments, schedules, etc. that works for you. You value others' time by being on time and showing up prepared and ready to go.
2. Respect your time and others. Arrive early and leave on time.
3. Communicate expectations up front, I can be there, I can't be there, I have an hour, etc. so everyone is on the same page.
4. The great thing about cell phones is they are mobile, so if you run into traffic, something comes up and you can't make it, call, or text and explain.
5. Keep in mind the work you are expected to do and the people you are serving and let this be your driving force to show up well.

Plan and Commit but Be Flexible

"Many plans are in a person's heart, but the advice of the Lord will stand."

Proverbs 19:21

To be strategic in walking out your purpose, planning is one of the best things you can do. Planning allows you to see what it is you are doing and helps you to determine how you need to make it happen. Planning can offer you time to reflect on where you have been and what you need to do to keep moving in the right direction. But even in your planning, you must be flexible. It would be unrealistic of me to instruct you to plan and stick to your plan without having the ability at any time to shift. The definition of the word "shift" is to – v. move or cause to move from one place to another, especially over a small distance. (Oxford Dictionary). So, when you determine a plan is not working and you need to shift, do it quickly.

I remember when my husband was teaching me how to drive a stick shift. That was a sad time because I didn't have the patience I needed at the time to make the transition from automatic to a stick shift. To ensure I remained independent and could continue to drive myself and the children to the places we needed to go, I had to learn . There was one time early in my training of driving a stick shift, I would take too long in shifting the gears. Every time I would delay shifting gears, I could hear the engine and transmission stalling (that's what I call it anyway), which was not good for the car. So, to keep from tearing up the car, I had to learn quickly to shift those gears. Same principle, when you realize a shift needs to be made by where you are in the process, shift quickly so you can keep moving.

The old saying made popular by Benjamin Franklin, "If you fail to plan, you plan to fail". This means you are not going to reach your goals and walk out your purpose by accident. You will need to plan your steps and even in that, God will establish them (Proverbs 16:3). Growth doesn't happen by accident and neither does walking in your purpose. As you plan, always remember, there are some things that will be out of your control, and they may delay your journey, but you always need a plan to get back on track.

Be Bold and Courageous

"Therefore, do not throw away your confidence, which has a great reward."

Hebrews 10:35

Your purpose is for you to complete. It is not for anyone else to walk in nor is someone else's purpose for you to walk in. I remember early when I began walking in my purpose, I was not completely confident in what I was doing. I always found myself learning and growing, but I found it very difficult to be comfortable in my walk and asking others to do the same. It was not until I began training regularly that I learned how important it is to be confident in my gifts. When I am called on for professional matters and situations, it's important to be confident in how I show up because people need what I have.

Showing up in a space with your shoulders back and your head held high, lets the audience know you are to be valued and the information you bring, will grow them. Now, you must make sure you do the work necessary. Don't just show up and expect others to appreciate you for just looking good! Look good and be ready to take them on a journey. Be ready to impact their lives. Your purpose is to impact the lives of others to hopefully inspire them to walk out their purpose and to remember something you have said. The way you can walk in a room bold, courageous, audacious, and unapologetically is by being prepared, knowing who you are and why you were created.

Have you ever been in a space with someone, and they are always apologizing for something, even if the situation in question was not their fault? Don't be that person. You should apologize for the things you have done wrong, but don't be wasting apologies on someone else's mishaps. Are you that person, who whatever the situation is, you are apologizing? This somehow makes you feel less confrontational or shrinks you in a room when you are feeling out of place. STOP! There is a time you would need to apologize if you made a mistake or missed a deadline or whatever the situation that was obviously your fault, but it isn't necessary for you to apologize just to be apologetic. Be strong and courageous in the work you are purposed to do. If you make a mistake, own it, and keep moving. Don't feel like you must shrink yourself in a room to be accepted. Be humble and strong. Remember, if you are in the room, you are supposed to be there. Bring your bold and courageous self, listen, learn, teach and be invited back.

Find Your Confidence in God

"For God has not given us a spirit of timidity, but of power and love and discipline."

2 Timothy 1:7

Valuing yourself and others is very important as you are living your life purposefully 1. It helps to keep your mind focused on the things you are called to and the people you are to serve. You will find times when you won't have a problem with valuing others, but sometimes you are not valuing yourself the way you should. There will be times when you will question yourself. You will struggle with believing that God has given you something others need, and you are the only one to give it to them. In that moment, you will need to rise up and think about all the times life experiences have educated you. Think about what God has allowed you to walk through and what you have learned on the journey. Having moments when you question your ability, but you continue to learn and grow, will keep you humbled and hungry to keep maturing in your faith (James 1:3). By remembering where you've come from and what you've been through, your spirit will rise with confidence and remind you of who you are and why you are here. Because you question yourself or your abilities does not make your value any less, so because you might think you don't have the expertise as someone else in the industry, doesn't mean someone can't learn from you. Again, shifting quickly will keep your negative thoughts from being fed.

Questioning yourself will remind you that your confidence must remain in Jesus Christ (Psalms 78:7) and all you are called to do, you are equipped to do.

Scriptures to meditate on and questions to ponder:

2 Corinthians 11:17, Galatians 6:7-9, Joshua 1:1-8

1. What is the most frightening thing about showing up unapologetically and courageously?
2. What does success look like to you and for you?
3. What do you think you will need to sacrifice to incorporate best practices into your daily purposeful living?

Chapter 10
DIFFICULT CONVERSATIONS

"You know this, my beloved brothers and sisters. Now everyone must be quick to hear, slow to speak, and slow to anger;" James 1:19

There will be times on your journey when you will have to have a difficult conversation. If you are where you desire to be in this process, you are probably reevaluating some relationships. You may be trying to cut away from individuals who have been toxic, but you've allowed yourself to stay connected. If you are wanting to continue to move forward, it may be time to have a difficult conversation. Please understand right now, not all conflict or difficult conversations are bad. When it comes to your important relationships, there must be some tension for the unnecessary fragments to be removed so the relationship can flourish. As scripture tells us, there is a way to have these very necessary conversations with relationships that matter most to you. The idea is that facts are needed, emotions are to be controlled, and opinions are kept at minimum. It will work, if you are "quick to hear, slow to speak, and slow to anger" James 1:19.

A few years ago, we had a very old washing machine. One day I put a load of clothes in and when I turned on the washing machine, it made an unfamiliar sound. Typically, when you put a load of clothes into the drum, add detergent, close the door, and set the temperature and wash cycle, you hear the cycle begin, water pouring in and the drum turning and it's doing its thing. This time, I set the cycle and began to walk away, then it happened. I heard a strange sound and came back, and nothing was happening. I stood there for a moment to see what I could see and noticed a humming sound; I lifted the door, and the clothes were dry and exactly the way they were when I put them in. I called the service person to come take a look, he checked it out and after investigating for a while, told me the agitator was out and he would try to order a new one. I asked him what the job of an agitator. He said that the component turns the drum and agitates the clothes, so they get clean. He continued to describe the agitator and how it works and said it creates tension/conflict between the clothes, so they get clean. This is the same idea with conflict and how it can move a struggling relationship toward a healthy one. There needs to be some agitation for the relationship to flourish. Conflict by its very nature is to help growth. Although there are opposing sides, the outcome should be good for all involved, if done correctly.

It is not customary for people to understand and realize the importance forconflict in growth but understanding that encouraging conflict does not mean you have to be at total and complete odds with someone. It means, coming to the table with different views and understanding as you move toward conflict, it is for a common goal or a common good. You may be at the point where you know something needs to be addressed for change to occur, but you're not sure how the other person might take it. This can cause some anxiety and make you feel hesitant to have the difficult conversation. It is not healthy to worry about things you cannot control. The bible tells us "And which of you by worrying can add a single day to your life's span" Matthew 6:27. Your focus must be on developing a healthy relationship for yourself, so you can continue to move forward with the level of support you will need. You must know what your needs are to be able to express them. As you are moving toward conflict, there are some things you must keep in mind for it to be a win/win for all involved. There are four things you should do when approaching a difficult conversation. When you are involved, you remain focused on the outcome, the reason why you are having this conversation in the first place, and how by having this conversation you are encouraging growth and intentionality. As you become more confident in having difficult conversations, start out by using these four suggestions, then move in your own comfortability.

Check Your Ego at the Door and Move Toward the Conflict

"For if anyone thinks that he is something when he is nothing, he deceives himself" Galatians 6:3

The first practical way to engage in a difficult conversation is to check your ego at the door while you are moving toward the conflict. You want to recognize the importance of conflict and how it can help your situation. You want to always be mindful of your word choice. And you don't want to seem as if you know everything.

The idea is not to hurt the individual you are engaging in conversation with but come from a place of genuine love for them (Romans 12:10). You want to make sure you are not instigating anger because of something you say or how you say it. It is important to check your ego at the door because you don't want to come across as arrogant but remain humble (Psalms 75:5). Approach the conversation in learning mode because you really don't have all the answers all the time and there may be some light shed on the situation by the individual as to why there's conflict in the first place. Keeping your ego in check, allows the other person to see you as valuing their opinion and will be more apt to open in the same manner.

Being mindful of your word choice is very important, again because you don't want the individual to take offense. Once a person feels offended, it's likely they won't hear anything you have to say. They will either shut down or get very angry and start attacking you because now they feel attacked. A way you can focus on your word choice is by saying things like: "I noticed that…so I was wondering if you needed my help with…" Or "I noticed yesterday when I said…your attitude changed. Did I say something or do something that caused that?" Asking questions this way will take the responsibility for action off the individual and place it on you and they should be able to feel your compassion. Checking your ego at the door, sometimes is very difficult for individuals to do because they are going into the difficult conversation from the standpoint of, "there is nothing I can learn from this person" or "they are trying to hurt me" when they may not have even pointed the arrow in your direction. Be humble and move forward. Take ownership for your wrong doing. Validate the individuals' feelings and express your genuine apology, if necessary.

Manage your Emotions and Define the Outcome from the Beginning

"A fool always loses his temper, but a wise person holds it back."
Proverbs 29:11

Next, leave your emotions out of it and define the outcome at the beginning of the conversation. This is important because you always want to be clear and make sure the other person is clear on why you are having the conversation. Everyone should be on the same page. If you need to dispel some untruth or ambiguity around the situation, this is a good time to do it before you get too deep into the conversation. Keeping emotions out of it. "A tranquil heart is life to the body" (Proverbs 14:30) and allows you to remain factual so you are not personally targeted. Define the outcome at the beginning so each of you know and remember what the conversation is about. Staying factual helps you to keep the focus clear and you don't lose sight of what you need to accomplish. This conversation is intentional so you don't want to waste time on unnecessary personal attacks, which can break down the relationship you have with the individual. If the relationship is already in a bad place and you are working on rebuilding, personal attacks will only make things worse.

Speak the Truth

"These are the things which you shall do: speak the truth to one another;"

Zechariah 8:16

Speak the truth based on fact not opinion. Approach the situation with themindset that you don't know everything and that this is a learning opportunity for you. This keeps compassion in the middle of the conversation. Remember this conversation is about addressing the facts only. While engaging, you may find the need to restate the purpose for the conversation. This is perfectly fine because although you try very hard to keep emotions out of it, they can creep in. Be mindful when you need to take a minute to redirect, calm, and start back up. If you move in this frame of mind you will continue on the right path to focus on truth.

Listen, Hear, and Validate

"A fool does not delight in understanding, but in revealing his own mind." Proverbs 18:2

Lastly, you want to make sure you listen, hear, and validate the other person throughout the conversation. Once again, restate the outcome at the end to make sure all involved understands what just happened. If necessary, stop the conversation (emotions may need a break), pick a time when to revisit. This break will give you and the other person time to think about what was said and how you can finalize things. Before the conversation is complete, restate the outcome and both of you determine if the outcome was reached to ensure the target was met.

Effectively communicating is important when moving towards conflict because you want to make sure you seek to understand. You listen and by validating the other person, makes them feel important and that you value their position. It also says that by validating the other person, you are saying you truly care about them and the role this relationship plays in your growth.

Because we live in an age where everything must be so fast and happen so quickly, relationships are expected to arrive in the same way. It is a process that you are progressing towards. Relationships are meant to take time, pour in, listen, learn, and apply. Having difficult conversations takes time to learn how and all parties will need to have the desire to move towards the conflict to establish a welcomed end.

Scriptures to meditate on and questions to ponder:

Proverbs 15:31-32, Ephesians 4:25, Colossians 4:6

1. Describe a time when you engaged in a conversation and allowed your emotions to control the conversation.
2. What are your thoughts about approaching a difficult conversation from the standpoint of "I don't know everything"?
3. Why do you think it might be difficult for someone to check their ego at the door when approaching a difficult conversation?

Chapter 11
MANAGING YOUR EMOTIONS

"Examine me, Lord, and put me to the test; Refine my mind and my heart."

Psalms 26:2

Emotional Intelligence (EI) has become a popular term over the past few years. Although there is a lot of information regarding it, I feel like the term is still difficult for people to understand. As someone living purposefully, it is important to understand the term and how it fits into what you must do to keep your focus sharp and your vision clear. Understanding your emotional intelligence and the impact it can play on your purposeful journey, is going to be important for you to grab on to. At any given point of your journey, if you are not aware of your emotional clarity and focus, you can succumb to moments of an unstable mind, body, and spirit.

Recognizing when you need to adapt and make some necessary changes so your response to life is an appropriate response in a healthy way, is key to managing your emotions well. The other thing about managing your emotions is how you respond to others' emotions can help others manage theirs. I remember watching a professional track meet with my husband and one of the athletes clearly was dealing with some unexpressed anger, but she was projecting the anger on anyone who was in her path. Like a dangerous tornado, she unapologetically whipped through whoever she felt was coming for her. Once the tornado died down, the aftermath of what had been done, mostly to herself, was very clear and unfortunately, some relationships were demolished.

Choosing to Forgive

"Be angry, and yet do not sin; do not let the sun go down on your anger,"

Ephesians 4:26

Has there been a time when you were most emotional about something, maybe a conversation or a situation that happened? You may not have had any control over the situation happening or how the individual involved reacted, how did you respond? Think about the last time you responded out of control. What emotions did you feel, anger, anxiety, frustration, stress? How did you respond, or did you hold it in, which also can have a negative impact on your mind, body, and spirit? Now that you have that picture in your mind, this chapter will give you a clear understanding of what it takes to improve your emotional countenance.

A heightened emotional intelligence is about knowing yourself, acknowledging your emotions, having the ability to control them, and the emotions of others. I truly believe that having the ability to let go and forgive immediately has a lot to do with how you go through life with your emotions in tack and serving others properly. The importance of forgiveness is crucial so you can move on with fulfilling God's purpose in your life. Having the ability to forgive quickly is a skill to be learned to drive away bitterness and resentment. To learn how to forgive, you must be able to receive forgiveness from God, forgive yourself, forgive others and be able to accept being forgiven. Without learning to forgive, your emotional instability will get in the way of you moving forward in purpose.

Here are six ways to begin your journey of forgiveness:

1. Go to God – "His word tells us to cast our cares on him because he cares for us" - 1 Peter 5:7
2. Lean into your emotions, don't act but acknowledge them (anger, hurt, vengeance) - Ephesians 4:26
3. Go with the process - give yourself time to process every step in the journey but forgive. It is required - Matthew 6:15
4. Set healthy boundaries – Psalms 16:6
5. Vengeance is not yours-so don't try to get back at the person – Romans 12:19
6. Pray for them – Luke 6:28

No one is saying forgiveness is easy, but it is necessary and required. If you follow these steps, they can help you move towards forgiveness. The biggest thing about forgiveness is that keeping an open mind to growing yourself and valuing yourself can lead you in the process. Forgiveness allows you to be in control of how you treat yourself and others. Forgiveness is also a character trait of Jesus Christ and in order for our sins to be forgiven, we must ask for forgiveness. It is not easy, but it is necessary. Keeping your focus on what you must do is imperative towards walking out your purpose. Living with unforgiveness can cause you to be stuck. You will find yourself wanting to move forward but can't until you address the unforgiveness in your life.

Harboring unforgiveness can make you reactive in your emotional space. You will find yourself feeling like you have opened painful parts of your life which can spark the unhealthy emotions that go along with that painful situation. Even in this, you must remember, by forgiving it does not mean that you will need to reconcile a relationship (especially if it is not healthy for you) and it does not mean that you must act as if nothing happened. It does mean that you have truly given that situation over to God and have released that individual or situation. You must let it go and not allow it to cloud your judgment or clarity in terms of walking in purpose. Forgiveness is for you.

If you hold on to unforgiveness, it can impact the way you handle your emotions. Moving forward, I hope you can see how continuing with unforgiveness in your heart, can make your journey unnecessarily more difficult. Move this obstacle out of the way so you can journey without distractions.

Improving Your Emotional Intelligence

"Do not be anxious about anything, but in everything by prayer and pleading with thanksgiving let your requests be made known to God."

Philippians 4:6

To improve your emotional intelligence, you must be able to manage not only your emotions, but the emotions of others. That might be strange to ask of someone, who only controls themselves. But think about it from this perspective. Think of those friends who cheer people up or who calm them down when they seem to be really upset or anxious about something. Experts would say, these individuals have a heightened sense of awareness and a high level of emotional intelligence. This can also be called empathy. Understanding where someone is coming from and being able to put yourself in their shoes and having the ability to express your understanding of their emotions, makes someone feel connected to someone else. I'm sure you have always known someone who has a gift in this area of empathy, or you may find it easy to empathize with others. It comes naturally for you or someone you know. Not everyone can empathize in such a way that it makes an individual feel and recognize, someone genuinely understands them. Effectively communicating requires some level of empathy for others to feel heard, valued, and validated.

It takes specific skills to improve one's emotional intelligence. Skills such as empathy, to harness emotions, and the ability to apply emotions to tasks like problem solving. While utilizing these skills, they also are managing their emotions and being able to regulate and manage others. Having the ability to manage others emotions may come naturally for some, but for most , this can be a difficult task. Try this, as you are talking with someone, and they express something where you clearly see their emotions taking over. Stop, look directly at the person, listen with your eyes and when they are finished, validate them and work to make them feel better. Work to manage their emotions while you listen and empathize.

To harness your emotions to problem solving, means that instead of allowing your emotions to overtake you and your entire thought process, you will use this energy in a positive way. Take a moment, breathe, or count to ten, think about what you can control. Determine if a shift needs to happen and do it quickly. What can be helpful is asking someone you trust their opinion on how to make something right. Use the information you have and create options to solve the problem. I always believe, having options is better than having one thing in mind and "two are better than one" (Ecclesiastes 4:9). What if that one thing doesn't work, then you must go back to the drawing board. But if you have thought out options, when you are in a situation where you need to pull from your toolbox, you will be well equipped to make the decision to solve the problem.

Asking good open-ended questions, will help to develop that emotional intelligence muscle. As I have redefined my fitness journey in my fifties, I am understanding the importance of rebuilding muscle. I think about working out and working to rebuild the muscle mass that it is said we lose starting at the age of 30, which is astounding to me. As I begin to rebuild muscle that I've so steadily been losing since the age of 30, I have to lift weights or incorporate some resistance in my exercise routine with consistency and regularly add more weight on the journey. Creating more weight and adding more resistance helps to develop muscle. The same general idea with improving your emotional intelligence muscle. You must continue to learn to manage your emotions and the emotions of others with practice and not shy away from problem solving or difficult tasks that may require you to be uncomfortable. That's what weight training does; you're creating pain in order to gain. During the process of weight training, you are tearing down muscle for it to be rebuilt. Building your emotional intelligence muscle means you will need to be uncomfortable with handling conflict, having difficult conversations, and facing obstacles full on.

Five Ways to Improve your Emotional Intelligence

"Finally, brothers and sisters, whatever is true, whatever is honorable, whatever is right, whatever is pure, whatever is lovely, whatever is commendable, if there is any excellence and if anything worthy of praise, think about these things."

Philippians 4:8

So, now that we have discussed what emotional intelligence is and the importance of forgiving and the role it plays in a healthy mind, it is important to know how you can handle situations better than you have in the past. You will be able to help others to manage their emotions. The thought of helping others with their emotions shows growth and your ability to have value in others by helping them to be more responsible with their emotions.

Let's review five ways to improve your emotional intelligence. They are: acknowledge, analyze, accept and forgive quickly, handle, and tell your story.

Acknowledge

Don't try to avoid your emotions but lean into them appropriately. Your emotions are not unimportant, learning how to operate when you are emotional determines how you show up. You will be creating muscle memory for the tough times. Understanding yourself and knowing how to connect to yourself and your emotions will help to improve your emotional intelligence well.

Analyze

Reflect and examine your emotions by doing what you need to do. By leaning into them appropriately, this can build strength, courage, know-how and you can continue to be aware and help others manage theirs. Ask yourself where the emotions are coming from and how you can best manage them in similar situations in the future.

Accept and Forgive Quickly

We learned the importance of forgiving and making sure you do it quickly. Accepting who you are and how you process is helpful. Acknowledging them for what they are and for who you are. You are human and your emotions are human emotions, so you are ok. God created us with emotions, so they are not bad, they just need to be managed. We were created in his likeness (Genesis 1:27) and they are very much a part of the human experience.

Handle Your Emotions

Find what works best for you and while you are managing your emotions, learn to handle the emotions of others. Others will see you as being helpful and valuable. Understand your experiences are valuable and so are you. Take time and step away to problem solve. Use a deep breathing method or count to ten to bring calm or redirect. Check in with one of your champions is a great option as well.

Tell Your Story

Use your emotional power to tell someone about what you are going through as you are walking out your divine purpose. Others need to see the vulnerable side of you, and this is how you will connect with them. We all have things God is working on and bringing healing to but in the midst of that, he has begun a good work in you and will complete it (Philippians 1:6).

Try to help someone this week manage their emotions and see how it makes them feel and you will feel great about how you were able to serve.

Scriptures to meditate on and questions to ponder:

Psalms 26:2, Colossians 3:13, Ephesians 2:10

1. Based on forgiving quickly, of the six practical tips on how to forgive, which ones do you find to be the most difficult for you to manage?
2. Describe a time when you have analyzed, accepted, and handled your emotions appropriately.
3. What is one thing you can do today to bring improvement to your EI?

Chapter 12
RUN YOUR RACE WITH CONFIDENCE

Ready

"...and let's run with endurance the race that is set before us,"
Hebrews 12:1

Get ready to explode to the next level. Don't stay where you are but be ready to explode. For you to explode, you must get into the blocks first. The race analogies come from my time around sports and being a runner. My children are athletes and my husband is a track coach, so many of my examples in life I get from athletic references, techniques, and descriptions. Well, this is another one, you must get in the blocks, first.

Being around track athletes for over twenty years now, I've learned enough to know that if you plan to go anywhere, you have to get in the blocks first. Once you are in the blocks, it is very important to be focused, intentional, and do exactly what you have been practicing. You must remember the technique, your form, and everything your Coach has told you in the process. Once the gun goes off, don't think so much, but allow your muscle memory to kick in and explode out of the blocks.

Set

"Be ready, and be prepared…" Ezekiel 38:7

You should be at the point, if you aren't already, beginning to take this position in determining where you go from here. You're in the starting blocks and positioned for an explosive take off. It is time for you to begin looking at your life and make some difficult choices. At this point, you should be ready to walk with no hesitation and audaciously into your purpose. Yes, with some fear still but walking forward and moving in the direction of your divine purpose. The only way you will be focused and intentional about walking full out, you must make some important decisions about removing the things in your life that are not benefiting you or your purpose (1 Corinthians 10:23). Coming out of the blocks explosively, will set you up for a successful race. In order to come out of the blocks explosively, you will need to move forward aggressively and intentionally. Doing this is what will make the difference in how you finish. Your strength as you step into your purpose will be evident based on how you have prepared and the race you have prepared for. You will then "rejoice like a strong person to run his course" (Psalms 19:5).

Go
Stay in Your Lane

"Therefore I run in such a way as not to run aimlessly;"

1 Corinthians 9:26

Having some skin in the game is one of those things we have always heard and pretty much live by when it is time to invest. Sometimes, we think investing in yourself only means monetarily. That is important but not the only way you can invest. There are moments you will invest your time, such as when learning how to walk out your purpose. You will also invest your gift. You will use your talents and gifts to move you closer to your purpose. Finding people to support and serve with your gifts is an important aspect of walking out your purpose.

When you explode out of the blocks and you are on your way, you have to stay in your lane. Why is this important? Staying in your land is important for a couple of reasons. One, so you don't impede another runner and two, so you won't be distracted by things that can hinder you or take your mind off of what is important to the goal. Staying focused on what you are called to do, also is how you partner with God to fulfill your destiny and allows his will to be done. Stay focused and don't look to the right or to the left (Joshua 1:7).

The Big Picture

"...but be transformed by the renewing of your mind, so that you may prove what the will of God is, that which is good and acceptable and perfect."

Romans 12:2

There are things that have attached themselves to you or you have attached to them, and you find that they aren't as beneficial as they used to be in your life. It may mean for this season and this moment; it is not working for you. You must determine if it is something you need to put away in a keepsake box in the top of your closet or if you need to get rid of it completely. The determining factor will need to be that thing that is either hurting you, causing you to hurt yourself, or keeping you out of the will of God. Then it is detrimental and must be cut loose. There was one time while I was in college, probably a sophomore. I met this guy who seemed to be so nice and different from anyone I had ever met and who had expressed an interest in getting to know me, so I thought.

We all have our stories of knowing someone who only expressed an interest in you because of what they could get out of the relationship. Well, I was a shy, young girl who didn't know a lot about people and didn't have a lot of experience with boys. In fact, he was my very first interest and I was a sophomore in college. I mean, I had high school crushes but nothing that I felt so strongly about. This young man was so charming and cute, and I was excited to get to know him.

However, it didn't take me long to figure him out and I have to say that was my very first adult decision to cut him out of my life. I am so glad it didn't take me long to make that decision. I learned very early, he wasn't good for me and where I was going in life. Shortly after that, I met the man I would fall deeply in love with, my husband, Stephen. Sometimes when you do the "big girl" or "big boy" thing and remove the thing from your life that you think is what you want, it opens the door for what God has for you. This is the same idea. Cutting things and people out of your life quickly is very important to your success in living purposefully and walking in the will of God. Honestly, anything outside of his will is not for you and understanding that sooner rather than later, can save you some drama.

With that being said in terms of cutting people off, know that when people walk out of your life, let them walk. From now on, do not try to hold on to toxic relationships. Trust in God to move people and things out of your life so his big picture can be fulfilled. Although we are relational beings, it doesn't mean you need to be connected to someone who is not good for you or is not aligned with your purpose. If you attach or connect with someone who is completely different from you in terms of your moral compass, you will open yourself up for pain and trauma that you can avoid. There will be some adjustments you will need to make but make the adjustments for you. Make the adjustments for the individuals you will impact with your purpose. Make the adjustment as quickly as possible or at least when it is made clear to you to do. The idea here is that you need to be so protective of your purpose, that you will not allow anyone or anything to interfere with its manifestation. Seek God in his infinite wisdom to help you regulate your relationships and any decisions you have to make.

God is the only one who knows everything (Genesis 41:39), so why not allow him to direct your footsteps and guide you in such a way that you will not regret your life choices (Psalms 119:133). Does this mean that you will always make the right choices, no that's not what it means? But what it does mean is that you will rely on God for guidance and understanding if you need to be cautious or make a slow connection. Don't waste your energy and time on a situation that is not going to be beneficial to where God is calling you. We only have so much time on this earth, and it should be about completing the work that God has given us to do (1 Chronicles 29:15). Stand on business!

Scriptures to meditate on and questions to ponder:

1 Corinthians 9:24, Hebrews 12:1, 1 Timothy 4:8

1. What are your next steps and who can you ask to help you?
2. What is the one thing you feel called to do in this season of life?
3. What can you do daily to move in purpose so you are standing on business?

All scripture references come from the Holy Bible translation of NASB 2020.

Follow me on Facebook at Melissa Cutter Roberts and Instagram @CoachMelissaRoberts.

For membership and courses with Living Whole Academy or to continue the

journey on achieving your goals, go to www.livingwholeacademy.com and sign up for the *Online Course Journey for Purposeful Living.*

To request for events, consultations, or training, contact me at Livingwhole20@gmail.com.

About the Author

Melissa C. Roberts is CEO of a nonprofit organization called Rahab's Women and Children Home, Inc. and walks in her purpose as an Author, Speaker, and Consultant. She has a master's degree in the Studies in Human Behaviors from Capella University and a Bachelor of Science degree in Criminal Justice from the University of North Carolina at Charlotte.

In 2012, while working as an adjunct instructor and Career Services Coordinator at Point University, she worked as a master's Level Counselor for the Touch of Healing Counseling Center, where she facilitated Grief Share small groups and conducted one on one coaching sessions. In 2017, Melissa worked as the Associate Director of Career Services at Clayton State University for three years. She now owns and operates Living Whole LLC, and works full time as a coach, consultant, and trainer. Melissa is also an adjunct instructor at Point University.

Through her coaching and consulting practice, Living Whole, LLC, she helps others view life through a wholeness lens to achieve a healthy balance of their mind, body, and spirit. As a consultant, she facilitates trainings, workshops, and webinars with organizations on professional development and honor (diversity training for faith-based organizations) training. She serves clients one on one by helping them

 to clarify their life purpose so they can achieve their goals. Melissa is the founder and editor of God's Whole Woman Magazine, an online publication, which encouraged women to live positive lifestyles in wellness, healthy living, self-care, and awareness. She is the founder of the Women Empowerment events which is designed to empower and inspire women to move out of the way of themselves to accomplish God's purpose for their lives.

As an Author, Speaker, and Training; Melissa is also an Independent Contractor Coaching for Runfast, Inc. and Ryse Athletics, LLC, both family businesses, where she coaches athletes on how to improve their emotional intelligence. Her online membership is called Living Whole Academy where she provides courses and produces a podcast called, Tea Time with Melissa.

Melissa resides in Griffin, Georgia with her husband, Coach Stephen "Stretch" Roberts, III of over 30 years. Stephen and Melissa have six adult children and two grandsons. Melissa enjoys spending time with family, traveling, watching movies, outdoors adventures, pleasing God and serving others by operating in dominion of what God has given her to do.

www.ingramcontent.com/pod-product-compliance
Lightning Source LLC
Chambersburg PA
CBHW050913160426
43194CB00011B/2382